SON OF ESCOBAR
First Born

Patrick Phillip Witcomb
July 1927 (Hull) - January 1993 (Surrey)
'Dad' a true hero

ROBERTO SENDOYA ESCOBAR

SON OF ESCOBAR

FIRST BORN

AD LIB

First published in 2020 by Ad Lib Publishers Ltd
15 Church Road
London, SW13 9HE
www.adlibpublishers.com

Text © Roberto Sendoya Escobar (Phillip Witcomb)

Hardback ISBN 978-1-913543-97-6
Paperback ISBN 978-1-913543-96-9
eBook ISBN 978-1-913543-90-7
ISBN 978-1-786751-12-6

A CIP catalogue record for this book is available
from the British Library.

Every reasonable effort has been made to trace copyright
-holders of material reproduced in this book, but if any
have been inadvertently overlooked the publishers
would be glad to hear from them.

Printed in the UK
10 9 8 7 6 5 4 3

Although this book is based on real people and real events,
many of those names, places and events have been
dramatised in order to tell the story.

CONTENTS

PROLOGUE

I had two fathers. The one I called Dad – and loved dearly – was my adoptive father, Patrick Witcomb. I knew him as an English businessman who had made a successful life for his family in Colombia. That was only half the story. It wasn't until years later that I found out he was also an MI6 agent working undercover for British intelligence. But hearing that still wasn't my biggest shock.

I learned that my biological father was Pablo Escobar, the most notorious gangster in the history of the world. I had met him only fleetingly, unaware of our connection – or that there were times he was prepared to kill to win me back.

This is the story of how the lives of my two fathers became inextricably intertwined.

Good and evil. Light and darkness. This story has it all.

When I was a child I knew nothing of all this. I just thought Patrick – Pat to everyone who knew him – was a regular dad. There were an awful lot of guns and strangeness going on around our beautiful mansion in Colombia but my dad worked for a firm that printed banknotes for governments and ran an armoured car business and as an employee he was subject to attack from criminal gangs. It was just part of our life, although sometimes it felt like violence followed us around and I was grateful for my round-the-clock armed protection.

There were also a few occasions on which my father took me to a place called Medellín where I met a younger man who took a keen interest in me – this was Escobar. And there was the day I saw huge bags of money being loaded on to a plane. Little did I know of the murky dealings that linked these two powerful figures in Colombia's turbulent history – and the millions of dollars that passed between them.

Only when I was twenty-four did my father – Pat – sit me down to tell me the true story of my extraordinary life. It was 1989 and by then I had left home and was living in Sotogrande on the Costa Del Sol of Spain, near Gibraltar. Until that day I had always been Phillip Witcomb, although I did know that I was adopted. It hadn't worried me. I always looked upon Pat and his wife, Joan, as my dad and mum. They had told me I had been born in Colombia, which explained my darker hair and features, but until this point both had said that nothing was known about my real parents and I had always accepted it. Now Pat prepared to turn my world upside down.

'What we told you wasn't the whole story,' Dad said. 'It's time you knew the whole truth.'

He revealed I had started life as Roberto Sendoya Escobar. They had adopted me from a Catholic orphanage. My mother was dead and they believed my father had given up any claim for me. It was then that he explained how he had come to cross paths with Pablo Escobar.

Dad had been tasked with setting up the Colombian arm of the banknote printing company De La Rue and, as part of his work, he needed to infiltrate the criminal gangs then gaining a foothold in the country's fledgling economy and pass back intelligence. Some of this information made its way back to UK secret services, but the main beneficiaries for the elaborate, sophisticated and devastatingly effective operation were their US counterparts in the CIA.

Dad explained that the armoured car division often came under attack and their consignments of newly printed Colombian banknotes would be stolen. After one such robbery, Dad received intelligence to the whereabouts of the missing money. With the backing of his bosses in London and his employers in UK intelligence he mounted a daring and heavily armoured mission to recover the cash.

It was in the course of this most bloody of expeditions that I was discovered as a helpless baby in the gang's hideout and the link with my biological father, Escobar, was established. At the time Pablo Escobar was a teenager and nothing more than a low-level criminal, but as he rose through the criminal ranks he would go on to be a useful asset for the intelligence services who sought to influence the growing gang networks in Colombia.

It was the 1960s and the cocaine trade was in its infancy. There was no way of predicting the way that its cultivation and supply would become one of the biggest industries in the world – or of knowing that the secret services would play a key role in allowing the gangs to flourish, creating the cocaine cartels that brought so much misery to so many people.

At the time Pat's goal was simply to safeguard his company interests and provide intelligence for the services back home. Enter one more figure who would much later become notorious on the world stage. An ambitious Panamanian, then just an officer, named Manuel Noriega, not only assisted Dad on the fateful mission that led him to Escobar but would also go on to help him in his dealings with the criminal gangs. Noriega and Escobar were quite the pair, between them overseeing the rise of narcotic trafficking to a global level.

What had begun as a low-level operation in aid of securely transporting government-issued banknotes exploded into a dangerous game: trying in vain to control drug gangs that nobody could have known would become so big that their resources started to outstrip those of many entire nations. Yet for years, US intelligence's attitude to the amount of cocaine flooding the USA verged on the relaxed. It was only when the amount of dollars for drugs pouring out of the USA – then the largest economy in the world – reached dangerously high levels, that action was at last taken.

The once primitive criminal gangs had by then morphed into huge drug cartels that made more money than they knew how to spend. By the time that I began to find out the truth of my life, Escobar was fearing his grip on power was slipping and had hidden millions of dollars in secret locations. When Dad told me all of this, and hinted that he knew where some of the money was, it was at first too much to take in.

It was only slowly that this incredible story began to make sense to me.

For years I had been plagued by vague dreams of what I thought were explosions and a woman's screams. Were these somehow related to real events, to that armed mission that Dad had mounted and that had led to my rescue?

I remembered our trips to Medellín. Suddenly, conversations I'd had with a mysterious man with a magnetic presence took on a new significance. Was this Escobar? My biological father?

Over the course of a number of conversations, I listened intently as Dad slowly revealed hidden details about my life. One part of the story was particularly hard for him to recount – the aspect I was most desperate to hear.

How had he known my biological mother was dead?

In explaining my birth mother's death, Dad shook me to my core, forcing me to question everything I'd ever thought I knew about myself, my legal guardians and the people who brought me into this world.

That wasn't all.

Many years later, as he lay dying, my father imparted perhaps his most sensational secret – clues to the location of Escobar's legendary missing millions.

What follows is based on the information given by my adoptive father, Pat, and blended with my own extensive research. This is at last the true story of my life. All the events are factual, although I have inevitably had to dramatise scenes and conversations as I believe they would have happened.

The story begins on the day that I was discovered by Pat. It was an accidental rescue that set the fates of Patrick Witcomb and Pablo Escobar on a collision course, bonding us together for ever.

CHAPTER 1: THE SECRET MISSION

Facatativá, Colombia, late October 1965

The two helicopters appeared with the rising sun.

Each spanking new US Bell UH-1 'Huey' was armed with two M134 miniguns capable of preset firing rates of 2,000 rpm, each linked to four thousand rounds of ammunition. They were also equipped with two M75 40-mm grenade-rocket launchers, both fed from a three-hundred-round magazine.

Aboard each were six newly trained Colombian special forces personnel. Sitting in the front passenger seat of the leading chopper was the man in charge. Pat Witcomb, a tall, powerful-looking Englishman, looked as incongruous as the two aircraft flying low over an otherwise peaceful countryside. They were three thousand metres above sea level, yet only five hundred metres above the ground. Pat could scarcely believe he was leading this mission. Before he joined De La Rue, a respectable banknote printer and security company established in London in the nineteenth century, he had barely set foot in a helicopter. Since then, the operations with which he had been tasked had grown increasingly dangerous. Almost of all of his training had been on the job itself.

He had swiftly discovered that Colombia was a violent country. Recently, one of his armoured cars had been blown up, killing two security guards and injuring others. This was one of the worst incidents to affect De La Rue, which had been tasked with securely printing Colombia's currency and transporting it safely around the country. The vehicle had been destroyed in the course of making a delivery and the incident had major ramifications for the firm. It wasn't just a question of the money that was stolen – although it wasn't an insignificant sum, running into the hundreds of thousands of dollars – but the message it sent out. The various gangs jockeying for power and influence would believe they could attack De La Rue with impunity and, by extension, they were hitting the heart of Colombia's economy itself. There had to be a firm response and once the firm received intelligence about the gang's whereabouts they were determined to strike back.

The pilot, sitting beside Pat, pointed to a cluster of dwellings on the hillside ahead. Pat compared the sight before him with the aerial photographs provided. He nodded. They were here. He glanced at the soldiers manning the machine gun and rocket launchers in the doorway and back to the other gunners in the second helicopter. He turned to the men behind, whose excited chatter had been constant since they left the country's capital city, Bogotá, and gave a thumbs-up. They clocked Pat's signal and, as one, fell silent, clutching their weapons in anticipation. Before they had set off Pat had thought the set-up he was commanding would be a sledgehammer cracking a nut and, as he looked again at the sleepy village ahead, his view was only confirmed. His targets wouldn't know what hit them.

'Hawk Two, this is Hawk One, over,' Pat said in clipped tones over the radio.

'Hawk One, Hawk Two, over,' came the accented response from his counterpart in the aircraft behind, a stocky man with a heavily pockmarked face. This was Manuel Noriega, then just an officer with the Panamanian military, but even at that point extremely ambitious. Seconded to the intelligence efforts in Colombia, he had been a useful ally to Pat in the shadowy meeting place where state business and private enterprise shared a common interest. Now Noriega seemed to be relishing joining in on the action.

'Hawk Two, we have visual on the target. Prepare to attack.'

'Roger Hawk One. Out.'

They dropped to a hundred and fifty feet and Pat gestured towards a small clearing ahead of the first house, radioing his intention to Noriega, who he always referred to by his codename 'JB', a reference to his favourite whisky brand, Justerini & Brooks. His eyes fixed on a rundown house with a single, small door to the street. Movement in the house next door caught his eye. Two shabbily dressed men appeared. He could see the terror on their faces as they scurried back inside.

The blast from the rotors kicked up a cloud of dust. As the choppers touched down, the soldiers jumped from the side and headed straight for the house. They only got a few yards when the two men reappeared in the doorway, this time with assault rifles. But before they had even cocked their weapons, a round of gunfire from the advancing troops floored them. More gunfire followed, as a face at a window was greeted with an avalanche of bullets.

'So much for minimal casualties,' Pat shouted to JB above the roar of the blades, as they took in the action, standing to the rear and flanked by two, blue-uniformed, close protection officers, or bodyguards.

JB shrugged. 'I told you, if they want a war, they'll get one.'

The soldiers split up into groups, some heading to the rear of the target property, others charging through the front door, while other units tackled neighbouring buildings. Gunfire resounded.

Pat respected his enemy as he looked around. They had chosen an unlikely hideout. Yet the response from the gang told him without a doubt that their intelligence had been perfect. It might look like a backwater – unremarkable farmer country – but this was one harvest worth fighting for.

JB and Pat advanced up the dirt track towards the building behind the security officers, their light, small-calibre submachine guns raised. There was movement from the back of one of the buildings. Another burst of rapid-fire gunshot. Two soldiers emerged with a large black bag. Pat nodded. He recognised one of the missing De La Rue-issue containers, exactly what they had come for. The thieves hadn't even bothered to switch the cash from the firm's own bags. He motioned to the soldiers to put it in the chopper and instinctively ducked for cover as shots rang out from somewhere behind him. He turned in time to see a group of around six men attacking from another building further up the track. No sooner had he spotted the threat than the gangsters were obliterated by fire from one of the helicopters. Pat paused to make sure no more reinforcements were on their way and dusted himself down before continuing his team's advance. This was turning into a bloodbath.

They stopped by the doorway into the house. From inside he could hear screams that chilled his blood. A protection officer stepped inside before returning to give him the all-clear. Pat and the others entered to see a man – or what was left of him – sprawled on the ground in a pool of his own blood. Astride him sat one of the Colombian soldiers with the butt of his gun rammed into a bullet hole in the fallen man's shoulder, screaming in his ear.

Pat could see it was obviously far too late for interrogation. He gestured to the soldier to step back. '*Muerto,*' he said – 'dead' – drawing a hand across his own throat to underline his words. The soldier composed himself and stood up. Pat needed to know if they had found any more of the stolen money. '*El dinero?*' he asked. The soldier shrugged but one of his colleagues had better news. Pat learned that more bags had been recovered, all filled with banknotes. They'd found a live target to question and he had given up the location of the rest of the loot and had identified his comrades. Mission accomplished, it seemed. This ragtag bunch of robbers and thugs might think twice before blowing up another of De La Rue's armoured cars.

A rattle of firing sounded from outside but then the guns fell silent and there was an eerie stillness. Only the hum of the rotor blades and the odd shout of '*claro*' – for 'clear' – came from outside. Pat wondered, Was anyone left alive?

JB seemed to read his mind for he shrugged and motioned to the security men to begin their investigation of the property. Pat paused to look once more at the corpse at his feet. Although bloodied almost beyond recognition the man looked young. Possibly still a teenager. He shook his head. Just kids. What were they doing getting involved in a man's business?

The blast of a single shot from another room gave him a jolt. Another fatal strike, probably. Their soldiers would have to be careful. So far, it seemed as if they'd managed to avoid any casualties. The last thing he wanted was some punk making a heroic last stand after pretending to be dead. He hoped they were taking nothing for granted.

A film of dust seemed to cloak the air. The day was not yet warm but he could feel his collar sticking to his neck and the moisture had dried from his mouth. He took out a handkerchief and mopped his brow.

JB and one of his security team took a room to the right while Pat moved through the rear of the house, where two steps led down to a back room. Gun still raised, the officer checked inside, gasped and took aim. Pat stepped from behind him and, on seeing his target, instinctively stuck out an arm to lower the weapon. 'No!'

There on the floor by a window was a woman, eyes wide, panting heavily. She was wearing what he thought at first was a red dress but, as he drew closer, he could see the crimson was not dye. He motioned the officer back and, ducking his 6-ft 4-in frame to enter the doorway, Pat approached her slowly, holding out his hands. As he did so, movement drew his eye to the corner of the room and to what he now saw was a cot. Sitting inside was a boy, all chubby cheeks and a shock of dark hair, staring back at him.

'Good God,' he said, kneeling by the woman. Her eyes were full of fear which at first he thought was probably directed at him and the harm she felt he might do her. He surveyed her injuries and began to suspect her terror was at the end she knew was coming.

'*Lo siento*,' he said softly – 'so sorry'.

'*Mi hijo*,' she said, her eyes watery, pleading: 'My son.'

'Ssh, don't speak . . . *tranquila*,' Pat said, suddenly finding himself having to search for the Spanish words that for the last six years had been commonplace.

He removed his flak jacket and tried to apply it to the source of the bleeding, a puncture wound in her side. She cried out as he gently eased her forward and it was then he realised that what he'd seen before was merely an exit wound. Shot in the back. *Christ*. He could only imagine what organs had been seared in the process. He rolled up the flak jacket and used it as a pillow, easing her back down on it. Even if he were able to get her on to the helicopter she'd be gone before they made it back to Bogotá. At least now her last breaths might be a little more comfortable.

She winced. Sweat poured from her brow, merging with the tears streaming from her eyes. She lifted one violently shaking hand. He could feel the effort it took.

'*Mi hijo*,' she kept whispering. He understood. My boy.

He clasped her hand but to his surprise she shook it free and then he got it. She was pointing to a small table with a drawer. He looked at it. '*El cajón?*'

She nodded. He shuffled over and pulled open the drawer. Inside was a small fabric bag containing what looked like keepsakes – a ticket of some description, a ribbon, a lock of dark hair and a much-folded piece of paper. As he inspected it, he saw her nod again. He unfolded it to see it was some form of legal document.

'*Mi hijo*,' she said again. She was looking into the cot, where the little boy still sat, smiling. She returned the smile, beaming, but it was too much for her and she broke down into heavy sobs, her whole body shaking now, her breathing laboured. Through her tears he detected only one word. 'Roberto.'

'*Si.*' He put a finger to his chest. 'Patrick.' He wasn't sure if she registered. He pushed the bag into her hand and tried to comfort her but she was fading fast. Her breathing rattled, he held her to try and calm the shaking. 'It's OK, it's OK,' he said, over and over but eventually he realised she couldn't hear him. She was somewhere else.

He laid the woman down on the floor and smoothed the hem of her dress down. He found a blanket over the cot and took one final look. She could have been sleeping. Only now, when she was at peace, could he see that she too was just a child, barely a teenager perhaps. He let out a long sigh and gently covered her. What was she doing in a place like this, a sparsely furnished room where the faded green paint was peeling off the walls? What a waste.

'Hey, what is happening?' It was JB. He was at the doorway with two soldiers. 'We should go. We got everything we came for.' He looked past the Englishman and clocked the body. 'Shame.'

'I'm coming,' Pat said. He looked at the child. What was he to do? This was not part of the plan. None of their intel mentioned the likelihood of collateral damage and they had not factored in human cargo. Yet he could not leave a child in this place; it would be to condemn him to death. He fished out the paper again. The woman, whoever she was, had wanted him to have this. She had wanted him to do something. The right thing. He saw a name on the paper: Roberto Sendoya Escobar.

Escobar? It was a name he recognised from one of the lawyers who had helped his firm set up in Colombia. He remembered what she said: 'Roberto.'

'So – you're Roberto,' he said, addressing the child. The infant smiled back. 'Pleased to meet you, too.' He gathered up the child in his arms and wrapped him in his bedding. 'You're coming with me.'

Later that day, Pat entered a Catholic orphanage in central Bogotá, carrying a bundle in tightly swaddled bedclothes. He asked to see Father Londono, whom he was assured would be expecting him. After a brief discussion Pat handed the bundle over to the priest, who bowed in recognition of his Christian act.

'I'll be seeing you,' Pat said, when it was time to leave. 'Take good care of him. *El es especial.*'

In the days that followed, news of the gun battle – and the heavily armed birds that dropped from the sky in the early morning sun, bringing mayhem in their wake and the deaths of everyone in what was supposed to be a safe house – spread from village to village. It would not have been long before word reached the ears of a fifteen-year-old boy, one Pablo Emilio Escobar Gaviria.

Few people would have known that he was connected to a victim of the raid. He lived 350 miles away in Antioquia and probably, like everyone else who heard the news, would have been shocked at first by the brutality in retribution for what had, essentially, just been a robbery, albeit one that had resulted in loss of life. When he thought about it, he might even have admired the ruthlessness of the operation. It was the sort of thing that would appeal to him. But then news filtered through about the young woman who died and the child she left in the house. Escobar had a brief relationship with her and knew the boy was his and that the child had disappeared. How did he feel about that? How did he feel when he found out who had taken his son? He would not have realised it then, but his life was never going to be the same.

CHAPTER 2: ADOPTION

Church of San Diego, Bogotá, December 1965

Amid the cacophony of cries, one rang out in the darkness. It cut straight through to the nuns' hearts, particularly to Sister Frances. She was not quite as old as some of the sisters but she had been there long enough to have heard it all – the cries of the fractious, the tormented, the downright difficult. As far as the nuns were concerned, every type of child had at one stage passed through the church, but few had heard cries like those of that little boy on his first night in the orphanage. Such was his despair she and others could only imagine the heartbreak he had suffered.

'Sssh, little Roberto,' Frances said as she soothed him. 'Your nightmare is over. You have nothing to fear now.'

The nuns had no idea what terrors had visited this little boy to make him shriek like that. They could only imagine what he had witnessed. Once calmed by Frances, he again became the cheery, good-natured child he had been when he'd first arrived. It was only while he slept that he became distressed. The nuns had only heard snippets of his story and how he came to be under their care at San Diego. Tales of terrible violence were common, usually confined to criminal vendettas, although the scale of bloodbath up in the hills prompted a discussion. Was Roberto's mother an innocent victim, caught in the wrong place at the wrong time? The nuns wondered what was happening to their beautiful country, when trauma on this scale was being visited upon such a likeable tot. And what about the boy's father? Had he been killed there? Why had he not been able to protect the mother or the boy? Did he even know his son was being looked after in the church? Would he come looking for him? Would there be people with guns? Many silent prayers were offered in the wake of such thoughts.

Little Roberto was certainly a special case, the nuns thought. He owed his life to the mysterious yet kind gentleman who had handed him in to the church. That fact alone was considered to be strange. Usually, when well-to-do people arrived at the orphanage – and others like it across the city – it was to take a child away. Under normal circumstances, babies of Roberto's gender, age and disposition were in high demand. They didn't even have to be orphans. The nuns had heard stories of children from poor families being sold and even stolen because rich people were willing to hand over so many American dollars for them.

Sister Frances bounced the little chap on her knee and he giggled in response. 'You are an angel, little one,' she said, smiling. 'Don't worry. You will be happy soon.' She already knew that her time with him would be brief. He wouldn't be staying with the other orphans for long. All the nuns knew it.

*

From his vantage point, eight floors up in the imposing Hotel Tequendama, Pat Witcomb looked down on the Church of San Diego across the street below.

'There you go.' His wife Joan, fair-haired and elegantly dressed in a tailored primrose blazer, handed him his drink, a large Scotch with ginger ale. He accepted it gratefully. After the day's events, he needed it. She took a sip from her usual – the same whisky mixed with soda.

'Still thinking of the boy?' She followed his gaze to the street below.

He nodded. He'd thought of little else since the events of that morning. No collateral damage, Noriega had said. Pat shook his head and sighed. For six years now, Pat and his wife had enjoyed the relative luxury of their serviced accommodation within one of Botogá's finest five-star hotels, yet during that time he couldn't escape the feeling that something had been missing. Perhaps that was about to change.

'Carlos is here to see you,' Joan said, touching his arm before moving towards the door of their lavish apartment.

The mood lightened as the jovial figure of Carlos Echeverri came into view, dressed, as always, in a suit and tie. The likeable Echeverri had once been an international statesman, serving as his country's representative to the United Nations and ambassador to Peru in a career that had not been without controversy. He angered his Peruvian hosts by granting asylum to a political rival of the president, sparking a military standoff. In person, Carlos seemed too charming and laidback to ruffle feathers but, as Pat knew, appearances were deceptive and Carlos had the right blend of charm and steel to make him a real asset in building relations. He had already proved extremely useful, acting as Pat's lawyer and advisor in cultural affairs.

'Señor Witcomb,' Carlos beamed, embracing the Englishman. 'How are you? A good day I hear.'

Pat nodded. 'We got the job done.'

'All the money recovered?'

Joan appeared with a drink for the lawyer and left the men to their conversation.

'Safely back in the company vaults,' Pat said, raising his glass to the lawyer's health. 'Mostly all accounted for.'

'Bravo! So the information was reliable.'

'Very much so.' Pat smiled.

'And I hear there was a little complication, no?' Carlos's brow furrowed.

Pat looked down again to the church below. 'You could say that.'

'You did an honourable thing, Pat.' Carlos clinked his host's glass in appreciation. 'Others might just have left the child to his fate.'

Pat shrugged. He led Carlos over to his desk and showed him the documentation he'd retrieved from the house. The sight of the artefacts that only that morning had belonged to a loving mother brought the images flooding back. He shook them from his mind. It didn't pay to dwell on what had happened. If he allowed them in, those memories of the woman and her red-stained dress could haunt him forever. What's done was done. He couldn't influence the past. But the future, he did have a say in.

Carlos studied the document. 'I understand don Gregorio has a lot to say about this?' he said.

Pat nodded. Gregorio Bautista was the entrepreneur whose idea it had been to bring De La Rue's international expertise to Colombia in the first place. He was also Pat's other close ally in this foreign country.

'What has he told you?' Echeverri said.

Pat leaned against the desk. 'He's extremely upbeat about the scenario. When I filled him in on what happened during the raid I don't think I've seen him happier. He doesn't see the situation involving the orphan boy as a problem. In fact, he called it an "unintended consequence, but an opportunity nonetheless. You would almost think that this was meant to be."'

'What do you mean?'

'He could see how troubled I was that we had left a child motherless. The woman was not much older than a child herself. The boy's father is either one of those killed in the house or he has long since given up a claim on the child. Gregorio is using his local contacts to try and establish the father's identity but he says it is highly unlikely that – even if he were to know of the child's whereabouts – he would want to take on such a responsibility. Given that Joan and I have talked about adopting a child, because of our situation, he thinks a solution might be right in front of our eyes.'

'And how do you feel about his suggestion?'

Pat glanced over to the window once more, thinking of the church below. 'I can see his logic. It could benefit us on many levels. All of us.'

'Splendid.' Carlos then lowered his tone. 'And is that a view shared by everyone?'

Pat looked over to where Joan was sitting, in her favourite armchair, reading a magazine. She had made her thoughts on the matter very clear. This was too soon to make such decisions. He was too emotional. He should allow time for the dust to settle and not rush into agreeing something just because Gregorio had suggested it. But Pat knew his own mind and knew when to trust his own instinct.

'Very much so,' he said.

Carlos looked again over the official document, running his finger over the lines, pausing at the boy's name and that of the mother. He stopped at the third name. Pat followed his finger to the name of the boy's father – 'Pablo Escobar,' Carlos read aloud.

'Is he going to be an issue?' Pat said. He was wondering if this 'Pablo Escobar' was a member of the same family as a man he worked with, Carlos Escobar, a financial expert who had been crucial in helping him set up his commercial enterprise in Colombia. When Pat had seen the name Escobar on what appeared to be the birth certificate, he had immediately thought of his banker friend.

Carlos shrugged. 'What does the banker say?'

'He thinks there might well be a family connection. He's looking into it.'

'Very well,' Carlos said. 'And what does don Gregorio say about the father, if there is a connection, or even if there is not?'

Pat hesitated. 'He thinks this "Pablo Escobar" could present us with another opportunity. He thinks Joan and I adopting a Colombian child could be good, not just for our wellbeing but in terms of cultural relations. And he thinks if this Escobar is connected to the gangs it might not be a bad thing for us if he also has this personal connection to our operation.'

Carlos nodded. 'Then leave the paperwork with me,' the lawyer said.

*

A few weeks later, a large, black, chauffeur-driven Mercedes pulled up outside the Church of San Diego. Out of it stepped Pat and Joan, accompanied by Carlos Echeverri and an armed bodyguard. Pat led the way into the church. Since his first visit he had been there many times, keen to check on the progress of the boy.

'He is thriving,' Father Londono had told him. Pat knew the nuns had taken special care of the boy and saw that one in particular, Frances, the younger sister, had taken quite a shine to the youngster. This visit was not a social one, however. He was now arriving on business.

The party strode in and made straight for Father Londono's office. The priest greeted Pat warmly. He looked pleased to see the Englishman had brought his wife. After a brief exchange of pleasantries, Carlos got down to the matter in hand. He handed over some documents to the priest and handed him a pen.

'If you will,' he said, softly but firmly.

Father Londono did not hesitate. Pat suspected this transaction must have ranked as one of the easiest the priest had to handle. He could only imagine the fates that awaited some of the other children. He was sure the church would always pray that their little charges found a happy home but he suspected those pleas were not always answered. He felt satisfied, however, that in this case, the right thing was being done.

'Excellent,' Carlos said when the formalities were concluded. 'Once these documents have been registered with the public records at the notary everything will be finalised.' To Pat and Joan he said: 'Congratulations. You are now the parents of a little boy.'

'Thank you, Carlos,' Pat said, exchanging a smile with his wife. Finally, he thought, after their own attempts had been unsuccessful, this was a second chance to start a family after nature, it seemed, had denied them the opportunity to have a baby of their own. In Colombian society, much stock was given to the family unit. A well-to-do couple could only go so far. The presence of a child, especially an adopted son of the soil, could do wonders for their status here. Not to mention that it would bolster his cover story as the boss of an international printing and security firm while helping to obscure his other line of work – gathering intelligence on criminal gangs.

Father Londono nodded. 'I have no doubt you will give the boy a happy home.' He clasped Pat's hands. 'God bless you for what you have done.'

On 7 December 1965, the adoption of Roberto Sendoya Escobar by Patrick and Joan Witcomb was officially entered in the public records of Bogotá, Colombia. With the death of the child's natural mother, a legal guardian had been appointed, a woman named Anita Uribe. Carlos Echeverri took on the role of her legal representative and it was Anita who was officially tasked with putting the boy up for adoption. It was all as Gregorio – confirmed in the paperwork as the boy's godfather – had said it would be. The boy's name was legally changed to Phillip Robert Charles Witcomb.

Four days later, the Witcombs returned to the Church of San Diego with their new son Phillip and the child was formally baptised by Father Londono. As was the custom in the staunchly Roman Catholic country, the boy was registered in the book of births and baptisms of the church alongside the names of his natural parents – Maria Luisa Sendoya and Pablo Escobar. It was and remains the only document in existence to confirm that Robert Sendoya Escobar, now Phillip Witcomb, was the first born child of a young man whose name would soon be known the world over. It would be many years before the boy learned of the dramatic circumstances that saw him removed from the loving arms of an impoverished Colombian teenage girl into a world where nothing was as it seemed.

After the baptism, the adoptive parents paid a visit to a nearby toy shop to buy their son his first teddy bear. Afterwards, Pat and Joan took him back home, which was now the apartment on the eighth floor of the Tequendama Hotel, across the road from the orphanage.

It would be some time before Pablo Escobar found out the truth about what happened to his son. Escobar, who had just turned sixteen on 1 December, was at the time of the adoption living in Envigado, a small village in the shadow of Medellín, nearly five hundred miles west from Bogotá. His parents were Abel de Jesús Dari Escobar Echeverri, a cattle farmer-turned-watchman and Hemilda de los Dolores Gaviria Berrío, a school teacher. They were not poor, by rural Colombian standards, and certainly educated, yet Pablo, the third of their seven children, dropped out of school before his seventeenth birthday.

At that age he had three passions; football, smoking marijuana and girls. After losing his virginity to a prostitute at thirteen, he thought he knew the ways of the world and had tried his luck with several girls, sometimes successfully. But that all changed when he met Maria Luisa Sendoya. Theirs might have been just another fleeting infatuation but very soon it turned serious. Faced with the persuasive attentions of an older boy who talked a big game, Maria might have found it hard to say 'No,' if she even did give her consent. She would only have been thirteen, a year below the age of consent in Colombia, but their union was a sign the young Escobar was already unaccustomed to having to wait for the things he wanted. He had already been involved petty thieving and the two young teenagers probably didn't pause to think about the legalities of consent. Maria, like many young girls her age, was seduced by the charms of this confident older boy. One can only imagine the shock, confusion and guilt she must have felt when, a few weeks later, she discovered she was pregnant.

In a deeply religious country, having a child out of wedlock heaped shame on the entire family of the mother. Abortion, a legal one anyway, was not an option. It was more common for the distraught teenager to be sent away to have her baby until a plan could be worked out to explain the new arrival. For Maria, that meant spending time at a remote hillside village west of the international airport in Bogotá. She may have felt isolated but, once her son was born, thought the only dangers lay in illness or prying local women asking too many questions. Never could it have entered her head that she and her boy were on a collision course with something as outlandish as foreign intelligence agents working to recover stolen cash from a British banknote company. But it was nonetheless the case that a secret operation, begun in London six years earlier, was destined to have tragic consequences for her and would the change the lives of the son she adored and the boy she'd inadvertently fallen in with from Medellín.

CHAPTER 3: THE ASSIGNMENT

Regent Street, London, December 1959

There was a bite in the air as the tall, smartly suited gent strode down the frosted pavement. He was on one of the capital's iconic shopping streets but it would still be some time before many of the stores opened their doors. As the man stopped outside the entrance to 84/86 Regent Street, he looked forward to the warming cup of tea he expected on his arrival. After several weeks on assignment in the baking heat of Pakistan, it was taking him longer than usual to acclimatise to the British weather.

'Morning Mr Witcomb,' the uniformed security guard greeted him on opening the door. 'Not seen you in a while. Successful trip?'

'Very much so, Davies, thank you. Good to see you.'

Even though he seemed to spend nearly as much time out of the country as on home soil, Pat was still on first name terms with practically everyone at the London headquarters of De La Rue. He had served in the air force and his previous job was with the police, where he marked himself out by using nightshifts at the station to study as a linguist. An ability to speak five languages was a valuable asset, as was his police training, and he had swiftly caught the eye of the enigmatic Arthur Norman, De La Rue's managing director and Pat had now been with the firm for five years. Initially, he was hired as a security advisor but his role had since changed beyond all recognition.

Arthur was a distinguished former RAF pilot who had served during D-Day and he saw something of himself in young Pat. He'd taken him under his wing, trusting him with special assignments designed to broaden his life experience as much as furthering his career. Now he was effectively a 'fixer', as Arthur described it – a safe pair of hands his boss trusted to send anywhere where De La Rue's interests had to be advanced and protected.

Under Arthur's stewardship, De La Rue had grown significantly from its colonial origins as a printer of playing cards, postage stamps and banknotes. It had become a modern, global industrial player, with a division devoted to security express couriering and another to armoured car provision. And its expansion into new markets provided the perfect cover for the British intelligence agencies – in particular MI6 – to keep tabs on foreign administrations. Arthur had left Pat in no doubt of the additional responsibilities that came with his role. The work of the firm came first but in close second position were the intelligence briefings that were passed on to the security services, both foreign and domestic.

Arthur, known to all his friends as Gerry, had also taught Pat the importance of discretion, and Pat had become reluctant to share details of his own personal life with anyone unless it was an absolute necessity. Like the hero of the James Bond books he'd devoured since their publication six years earlier, Pat liked to remain inscrutable.

He avoided small talk as he arrived at the Regent Street offices, where he had been summoned by Arthur, and he didn't need to be shown where to go. As he exchanged the briefest of pleasantries with the rest of the security team inside the lobby, a familiar face came into view. Lady Anne was Arthur's immaculately presented, middle-aged personal assistant.

'Lady Anne,' Pat said, striding forward as she emerged from an elevator. 'How good to see you.' She offered both cheeks for him to kiss. 'You're looking well,' he said, stepping back to appreciate her. 'Tuscany, was it?'

'Kind of you to remember Pat, yes,' Lady Anne said, gesturing her companion to the lift. 'Lovely. And all too brief.'

'How's business been?'

'Challenging, as always.'

'And how is Gerry?'

'The same,' she said, smiling.

Lady Anne – so called because of her aristocratic heritage – might have been officially the managing director's trusted and loyal assistant, but Pat had long acknowledged that, effectively, she ran the operation. He watched as she used a buttoned panel to summon an elevator. The lift doors opened and they headed for the top floor, emerging into an oak-panelled lobby office lined with filing cabinets behind a large, mahogany and leather desk. Lady Anne led Pat towards a door thick enough to provide effective soundproofing. On the other side was Arthur's office.

'Patrick, good to see you, old boy.' Arthur, looking splendid in a newly tailored suit, strode towards Pat and offered a firm handshake.

'Gerry, how are you?' Although it had only been a few weeks since they last met, Pat detected fewer hairs on his boss's greying head.

'Good, good. Pleasant trip back?'

'It was OK. We —'

'Good, good. Have a seat.'

Pat exchanged a smile with Lady Anne. Arthur was known for his brusqueness and rarely tolerated small talk.

The cup of tea – Pat had been dreaming of it since that dreadful train journey to Islamabad on his last assignment – duly arrived, along with an array of rich tea biscuits. There's nothing quite like home, he thought, as he sat down in the old, large, green leather Chesterfield, his usual spot in Arthur's office.

Although a product of the English boarding school system, Arthur was no silver-spooner. At Blundell's, where he had been head boy, the motto was, 'For the country and the people' ('*Pro patria populoque*') and this was something he still lived by. He had worked his way up the hard way but now, as the steward of Britain's leading blue-chip security firm, he had privileged access to politicians, diplomats, security chiefs and intelligence agents, such was the nature of the information his company controlled in its foreign endeavours.

Pat had barely taken a bite of a biscuit when Arthur sat back on his chair and nodded to Lady Anne. She leaned over and pushed a button on the right-hand side of his desk. The curtains drew shut as the lights dimmed and a screen lowered in front of the oak-panelled wall opposite the window. The room filled with the sound of a revolving movie reel. A black-and-white, 8-mm home movie depicted several men talking on the terrace of a large house with views of what appeared to be countryside in some other country.

Arthur explained that he had received a request from a contact in Colombia. A British embassy official had been approached by a leading businessman through 'our American friends'. He pointed to a short, stocky man in a pinstriped suit. That, Arthur said, was Gregorio Bautista, the businessman who, through his intermediaries, had contacted De La Rue's American intelligence contacts. Bautista wanted the company's help in setting up a secured armoured car division and, ultimately, a banknote printing business. Colombia, Arthur explained, was a largely lawless place and the authorities hoped the outside security could assist in legitimising the government.

Arthur said his American intelligence contacts viewed the request as an opportunity. The country was in a state of political unrest, putting off many foreign investors. Indeed, there had even been recent trouble in the Colombian capital, Bogotá, involving local smugglers from the second city of Medellín. Arthur said the Americans requested a Spanish speaker – someone with experience of running both a commercial security and armoured car operation – and an intelligence detail to be sent to offer advice. Pat was that man and his instructions were to go to Bogotá, meet up with Gregorio Bautista, find out what he wanted, speak to the firm's US contacts and report back.

'It'll be a long trip, 'Arthur said, 'so take Joan with you. It will be good for her to get a feel for Colombia. Anne will make all the necessary arrangements.' Pat nodded and focused once more on the movie, which was now showing a scene shot outside a vast red brick building. 'That's where you'll be staying, the Hotel Tequendama, named after the famous waterfall. It's where all the military stay so you and Joan should be perfectly safe there while you find out what this is all about. Any special instructions will come through the embassy telex in the usual code,' Arthur said as the clip finished, in a tone that told Pat the meeting was over.

Days later a British Overseas Airways Corporation (BOAC) Boeing 707 departed from London Heathrow on its regular, midweek South America run. Among the first-class passengers were Pat and Joan, to the casual observer just another couple on a business trip and, had anyone been curious, they would have been told the pair were visiting several Latin American countries with a view to obtaining contracts to provide security and printing services. Pat's executive position within a global corporation always gave him a plausible explanation for his travel plans and he was adaptable to the demands of De La Rue. Joan worked for a high-ranking official in the Foreign Office and she too understood perfectly the demands made by the employers in their particular field of overseas work.

Pat even had an advantage over a fictional spy such as Ian Fleming's James Bond, who had to rely on the cover story that he worked for the international trading company Universal Exports. Pat didn't need to worry about anyone unearthing a sham firm story; he just had to make what were entirely legitimate enquiries on behalf of De La Rue and, when something arose that he knew would interest the intelligence services, he would pass it on.

This latest assignment involved an eleven-hour, soul-destroying journey that stopped in Antigua, the Caribbean, and the Venezuelan capital of Caracas. By the time the flight eventually touched down in Bogotá the couple were exhausted but sleep would have to wait.

Along with a blast of warm, dry air, an official met them as they stepped from the aircraft and escorted them through a side door that bypassed the regular passenger customs and immigration area. There an American man met them. He introduced himself as George Williams and Pat knew him to be one of the CIA's men in Colombia. George ushered them to a black Chevrolet. Heading into the city centre, the stifling summer haze immediately clawed at their throats. Pat gazed from his window and got a first taste of the Bogotá motorist, a breed of driver to whom any kind of highway code was an alien concept. He marvelled at the multi-lane crossroads where a solitary policeman, armed with only a whistle and a collection of hand signals, somehow kept order. It was like a chaotic ballet, Pat remarked to Joan, as the otherwise manic drivers danced to the officer's tune without collision.

At the hotel, the couple were shown to their three-bedroom serviced apartment. Pat took a brief moment to appreciate his surroundings. The luxury accommodation was like an oasis of calm amid the frantic pace of the streets below. He noticed a charming church across the road, another incongruous sight next to the busy intersection. The blast of horns and music coming from beautifully painted buses were in complete contrast to the orderly London streets he'd left behind. He looked around at the state of the buildings and roads and, even though he'd only recently been in under-developed Pakistan, he couldn't escape the feeling that he'd landed in a place where, aside from the volume of traffic, time seemed to have stood still for fifty years.

'I imagine you're keen to know what this is all about,' George Williams said.

Pat nodded. 'It would help.'

'Don Gregorio is a good man. When you meet him, he will impress upon you the need for your company to come and set up a legitimate business here.' Pat could sense a 'but' coming. 'But, the reason we are involved is that having you guys here could provide a perfect opportunity.'

'For what?'

'To infiltrate criminal gangs who, if left unchecked, could further destabilise an already volatile country and pose a threat to American interests.'

Pat smiled inwardly at the mention of 'American interests', a phrase that was designed to mean anything.

George explained that the gangs were starting to produce substantial quantities of cocaine, then a drug almost unheard of in the UK. It was imperative to infiltrate these outfits to get control of the cash flow. 'It will require close cooperation between agencies,' he said. 'There are a few interested parties involved here.' Pat wanted to know more about the production of this drug 'cocaine' and George gave him a history lesson. For centuries Colombia, a stunning country, had been populated by various indigenous tribes, most notably the ancient Muisca civilisation, whose way of life centred on the rural village and subsistence farming in the foothills of the Andes. The environment provided the ideal growing conditions for the coca plant, which grew over vast swathes of the country. Chewing its leaves was a pleasurable pastime that became indispensable, particularly for men. Humans being humans, someone had come up with a way of processing and packaging this addictive substance as a marketable, recreational product. Its popularity was spreading from rural communities to the cities and was now reaching beyond Colombia's borders.

'That's enough for now,' George said, 'You'll hear more about this very special country from Gregorio. Take your time to settle in and, when you're ready, call the embassy and they'll have someone collect you.'

No sooner had George departed than Pat picked up the phone to the US embassy. In a matter of minutes, a knock at the door signalled it was time to head to the lobby. Two officials flashed their US ID cards by way of introduction. They showed Pat to a waiting Willys Jeep. A uniformed officer saluted and opened the front passenger door. In an instant the doors slammed shut simultaneously and they sped off through the mid-morning traffic.

Still dressed in his Savile Row suit, Pat felt slightly self-conscious but his extensive experience in foreign countries told him that the more sophisticated the look, the more disarming the effect. Few people suspected the man in the suit, even when violence, espionage and all manner of dirty tricks followed in his wake. If anyone accused Pat of stirring up trouble, he would explain: when you are in the business of transferring currency and providing armed security, you become a target and it is inevitable someone will get hurt if interested parties come at you with guns.

After a short drive the Jeep arrived at the entrance to a well-defended compound, the American embassy. Once through security, they were to have a meeting in offices on the third floor, an area that was sparse and, Pat noted, not at all like Arthur's cosy snug. Pat's minders guided him to a large square briefing room, where a short, stout Colombian in a navy pinstriped suit greeted him.

'Señor Witcomb,' the man said, extending a hand. He continued in faltering English. 'Gregorio Bautista. Thank you for coming all the way to Colombia to help with our small matter.'

'Don Gregorio, what a pleasure it is to meet you,' Pat said in fluent Spanish. 'I am here to assist in any way I can.' Gregorio gave a smile that Pat took to mean his response had been the right one. The Colombian was keen to get down to business – a man after Arthur's heart, Pat thought. As Gregorio spoke, he confirmed what Pat had been told – that this was a country with more than a few security issues. Gregorio underlined that the authorities needed De La Rue to bring their banknote printing business and armoured car service to Colombia for the nation's government.

'I can assure you we will reward you and your company.'

Pat offered a tight smile. He found the offer of bribes unnecessary. Once they began working together his new Colombian colleagues would find that, when dealing with the British of De La Rue, a polite gesture was usually enough.

Gregorio welcomed other experts to the meeting, including representatives of the military, who explained to Pat the peculiarities of a country that was the size of France and Spain combined but had very poor infrastructure, creating conditions that allowed bandits and criminals to thrive. Colombia was still recovering from *La Violencia*, a ten-year civil war sparked by the assassination of popular presidential candidate Jorge Eliécer Gaitán and fought in the provinces. It had only officially ended the year before and brutal, violent murders were still commonplace. Colombia continued to be a wild and dangerous place where it seemed the value of life was measured in pesos. Communities would regularly wake up to a plethora of corpses randomly abandoned from the previous night's round of vendettas. Bogotá was no exception. The military men explained that a cultural fondness for lawlessness meant that imposing the rule of law was challenging, to say the least. The arrival of De La Rue, with its international know-how, was invaluable to a government keen to establish its authority by any means possible.

The meeting ended late in the evening and Pat thanked the participants politely – as if their contribution had made a significant difference to his final decision, which was to report back to London before doing anything else. In don Gregorio he found someone who clearly knew what he wanted and how to get it done. Pat stepped back into his chauffeured Jeep with much to ponder. If the firm were to be tempted it would require a lot of money.

On the way back to the hotel, Pat asked to stop off at one of the many flower stalls along the roadside. Persuading his wife that they were going to have to face the arduous journey back to London almost immediately was not going to be easy. He arrived back at their apartment to find that, while he had been at his meeting, Joan had already built up quite a collection of brochures and was already planning her sightseeing tours. Unfortunately, playing the tourist would have to be for another visit.

*

Back in London, at his first opportunity, Pat reported to Regent Street.

'How did you find Colombia?' Arthur said, greeting him with the customary firm handshake.

'Brief,' Pat said, smiling.

Arthur laughed. 'What did they make of you, a gringo in their midst?'

Pat shrugged. 'I'm sure they've met worse.'

'Quite.'

Pat couldn't tell if Arthur was joking.

'And what did you make of Gregorio?'

Pat paused. He might not be able to gauge his boss's humour but he always knew when Arthur was testing him. 'He struck me as someone we can do business with,' he said.

'Excellent, now come with me.'

Arthur strode out of his office and to Lady Anne, who had been waiting outside, he said, 'We are going to the club for lunch with some . . . friends.' Pat knew 'friends' was code for 'contacts' – those with the skills to facilitate setting up De La Rue enterprises in Colombia.

Arthur's black Daimler was outside, engine running. Pat smiled. He knew the managing director demanded his driver have the car heated to exactly the right temperature before he entered. Arthur hated the cold – this winter morning was particularly bracing.

'I like this chap, Gregorio,' Arthur said, once he, Pat and Lady Anne were settled inside.

'You've met him?' Pat said.

'Once or twice. He's been over here to visit a few times.'

Pat nodded. He had suspected his little fact-finding mission to Bogotá had been more for his own benefit than for Arthur. He also suspected that the requests for help he'd heard in the American embassy would only cover a fraction of De La Rue's future role in Colombia.

Arriving at the private member's club in Mayfair, they were shown to Arthur's favourite table, set for five. Arthur introduced them as Alan Mitchell and Michael Carr from the firm's printing division. Lady Anne handed Pat, Alan and Michael each a thick file.

'Considerable investment is about to be made in Bogotá to establish a printing works,' Arthur said. 'If we are to produce newly printed banknotes in a land where crime is rife we will need to have a security operation in place. It will be impossible to guarantee delivery to the banks using third parties. So, we will have our own an armoured transportation business alongside the printing operation. You will have a significant budget, not only to oversee the set-up of the secure printing business, but also to engage in the procurement process for the armoured cars. Pat, it will be your job to oversee it all. You will liaise with a contact of mine from the Colombian army, a Colonel Savogar. He will provide you with the weapons you need.'

Pat had a quick glance at the file. It contained an in-depth study of the project, along with budgets and forecasts of expected growth; material that could be left to the other two.

'Colombia presents a challenge different to any we have faced,' Arthur went on, channelling, it seemed to Pat, his inner Churchill. 'Nevertheless, failure is not an option that will be accepted under any circumstances. This is an extremely sensitive yet potentially extremely lucrative venture. The very fate of the company is on the line.'

Pat had heard such rhetoric from Arthur before, however, he did acknowledge there was a slightly different tone to the chief's voice. More was to come, he thought. As lunch was served, they discussed the basic parameters for working together. Gregorio would help the team on the ground with anything they needed – and this meant absolutely anything. As the meal concluded, Arthur declined his usual brandy, saying he needed to get back to the office. He asked Pat to accompany him, saying there was time to drive him to his home in Finchley, north London. Pat knew one of Arthur's confidential chats was coming.

'As you have gathered,' Arthur said in hushed tones, though a screen separated them from his driver, 'running alongside the printing division will be a secret operation. There is someone else you will meet,' Arthur's voice was now a barely audible whisper, 'a Panamanian military officer, an agent for the CIA, will work with you on special contracts. His name is Manuel Noriega, codenamed "JB".' Panamanian military? Pat was beginning to understand what the American George Williams had meant by 'interested parties'. 'Your main mission will be to facilitate the secure transportation of funds from certain private clients.'

'Private clients?'

'Coca-producing gangs.'

'I see.' Pat was beginning to understand now.

Arthur said, 'If we can infiltrate one of the main smuggling gangs by offering to be a cash carrier, we should be able to track the cash to its final destination. The Americans are growing increasingly concerned at the growth of these operations. This venture will allow them to follow the money. You can take it as read that this will be classified as a K-notice operation.'

Pat didn't need to have it spelled out. A K-notice was 'plausible deniability'.

'For reasons unclear the operation will be called "Durazno".'

'Peach?' Pat said.

'Pardon?'

'Peach. "*Durazno*" is Spanish for "peach". Is there a connection?' Pat immediately regretted his display of knowledge. He knew Arthur hated it when it looked like anyone was smarter than him.

'Durazno's primary function,' Arthur went on, ignoring the interruption, 'will be to provide intelligence for the main American counter-insurgence operation set up by the CIA earlier this year. Obviously, from time to time, in some cases, you will have to deal with some unsavoury characters. Nothing you can't handle, of course, given your experience. Given the nature of this operation, the fewer people who know about it the better – especially not your new friends in the printing division. It's up to you, of course, but you might not want to divulge too much even to Joan. Her presence by your side will provide valuable cover.'

'Sounds interesting,' Pat said.

'Doesn't it?' Arthur eyes lit up. 'I'm almost jealous I'm not giving it a crack myself.'

Pat smiled. He could well imagine. Over whiskies at the club down the years, Arthur had regaled his younger employee with tales of how, twenty years earlier, he had been sent to Shanghai to run a similarly secret operation printing banknotes for Chiang Kai-shek's nationalist government, under the noses of occupying Japanese forces. He helped set up a printing plant disguised as a playing card factory and told Pat how they smuggled in watermarked paper and printing plates and hid the finished product in dustcarts to avoid detection. When the Japanese at last intercepted a consignment of paper money and demanded it be burned, Arthur offered to do so himself. Away from watching eyes, he salvaged half and managed to deliver the banknotes using his own car. Then there were his wartime exploits – his heroics as a pilot earned him a Distinguished Flying Cross for gallantry against the enemy in the air.

Pat respected having a boss who would never ask him to do something he wouldn't be prepared to do himself. Yes, this was a new challenge. The drug business was an unknown quantity, but he had dealt with smugglers and pirates in other countries. He'd found a fine line existed between the most successful businessmen and the most effective gangsters. There was one thing he wanted to know: 'What of Gregorio?'

'I imagine he is looking at the wider political picture and playing a long game. A business venture of this magnitude will provide the financial muscle to deliver real political power in a backward country like Colombia. After all: he who controls the cash controls the country.' As the car arrived at Pat's flat, Arthur handed him another file, marked 'top secret'. Pat noticed some other symbols on the front – 'M10 . . . . one / .6s. = 6.°'. 'Some additional information,' Arthur said.

From his time in the police, Pat recognised masonic code. They must really want to keep this secret, he thought. He bade Arthur farewell with many thoughts spinning around his head. Practicalities: how was he going to explain this to Joan? They would be out on a permanent posting. She was going to have to give up her job at the Foreign Office. This was going to be nothing like any other mission he had undertaken. They were going to have to entrench themselves in the upper echelons of a foreign society on the other side of the world. They would be creating an endless whirlwind of public relations engagements, embassy parties and corporate functions, all of which would be in aid of achieving the takeover of another country's monetary system.

This was without allowing for Operation Durazno itself. He was starting to think it was an operation aptly titled. On the outside it looked to be a very attractive and tempting business proposition with sweet and extremely juicy financial rewards, while at its centre lay a hard stone.

*

A week later Pat was on his way back to Colombia on another BOAC South America flight. After heated discussions, it was agreed Joan would follow him at a later date, as she had to keep an eye on her elderly mother, who lived not far away from the couple in London, in Swiss Cottage.

Travelling alone suited Pat. He could get his teeth into his new role; immerse himself in the assignment without distraction. He took up residence once more on the eighth floor of the Tequendama Hotel in the serviced apartment. One of his first tasks would be to act as signatory to the new trading account at Colpatria Multibanca SA, a bank that was part of the Scotia group, which had long-standing connections to De La Rue. Gregorio made all the necessary introductions.

One of the bank's directors ran the De La Rue account personally, Carlos Escobar. He came with outstanding credentials: an economist at the Universidad de los Andes, he was also a managing partner and legal representative of Corredores Asociados SA and a stock broker with other financial interests. As a senior banker, he wielded a great deal of influence in his country's financial community and was someone Pat would grow very close to, both on a business and a personal level. He would go on to help De La Rue secure contracts from other banks to transport their cash and it was he who would be instrumental in supplying the contacts for moving money that wouldn't be declared so readily on the company books. This very respectable banker would also be one of the two principal witnesses – along with Gregorio – on the adoption certificate of the young boy who was to be taken in by the Witcombs. But to the young Phillip he would be more simply known as Uncle Carlos.

CHAPTER 4: THE DARING PROJECT

Medellín, 1966

No one gave the solidly built teenager with the large holdall a second look as he crossed the busy street. If they had, they might have seen the barrel poking out of the bag. The boy got to within a few steps of the building entrance – there was no going back now. Even to pause would be to fail. And he would not do that. He was committed. Any last nerves or twinges of disappeared as he opened the door. Once inside the bank he looked, to witnesses, strangely calm, as though he'd done this a thousand times.

Approaching the first cashier, he opened the bag, pulled out the borrowed rifle, lifted it to his shoulder and pointed it straight at the startled woman.

'Nobody move,' he shouted, repeating what he'd heard in countless movies. 'I will start shooting if you don't fill this bag with money.' To his satisfaction, the tellers jumped into action, pulling out drawers and stepping forth with bundles of notes and bags of coins. Holding the rifle with one hand, he passed the bag to the cashier and, as she stuffed it with cash, he glanced around the bank. There were only two or three customers. They all stood in stunned silence, waiting to see what he would do next. 'That's good.' He directed the cashier to her colleague who had found a bag of notes. 'She's got some more for you.' When the bag was full, he took it back and waving the rifle in the direction of the customers, walked back out of the bank.

Outside, he would have been pleasantly surprised to see everyone was going about their business as normal. He couldn't have believe how easy it was. He had in his possession more money than he had ever seen in his whole life. Later, when he dwelled on the cashiers' frightened expressions, the shocked faces of the customers, he sensed the power his actions had given him. It would be a feeling that he got used to having.

When he next tried a robbery, a few weeks later, he appeared even calmer than before, this time chatting with cashiers while they hurriedly stuffed notes and coins into his holdall. Some might have said he was cheery. He even thanked them on his way out.

The bank jobs brought him wealth and status, admiration from peers and greater success with girls. In Medellín, the 'city of everlasting spring', where the climate remained a pleasant 20–30°C all year round, a reputation was blossoming. The name Pablo Escobar was already known in connection with petty street robberies and selling fake lottery tickets and contraband cigarettes but he didn't just want to survive on those skills for the rest of his life. He had big dreams. He told anyone who would listen that he wanted to be a millionaire by the time he was twenty-two. If that was to happen he – along with his cousin and long standing partner in crime Gustavo Gaviria – had to keep raising their game.

Just as he'd got bored with those early ventures, the teenager soon began to crave crime that was more sophisticated and dangerous than bank jobs; something that came with even greater rewards. He had to keep thinking big and got involved with a gang who, among other robberies, had held up the new armoured vehicles that had been seen on the streets of Colombia.

*

Across the country in Bogotá another reputation was growing. Since he'd arrived in Colombia, Pat Witcomb had barely stopped to catch breath. With the Colombian banking details for De La Rue settled, he moved on to identifying a location for the company headquarters, somewhere that was large enough to house a printing works and secure enough to act as a base for the armoured cars. Given Colombia's troubled history, just getting a company of the nature of De La Rue off the ground was a significant achievement – a daring project even. It would be Colombia's first step into a modern, more sophisticated world.

A large vacant building on the Avenida de las Américas met all of Pat's requirements. There was adequate room for the printers, along with garages and a significant yard able to accommodate at least twenty trucks. Pat took an office on the second floor and Gregorio, as his close working partner, was close by. Liaising closely with the team Arthur had assembled in London, the company had everything in place for the printing plant's launch in 1961. Within two years and thanks largely to Gregorio's contacts, Pat established the armoured car side of the business. As he had planned, everything operated from the same site. The vast printing works had a permanently manned security office that served as a secure entrance and exit for the armoured trucks that moved cash and gold. Lucrative contracts were soon established and everything seemed to be falling into place. Pat was the managing director of De La Rue, Colombia and Gregorio was its founding president.

Arriving a few weeks after Pat in 1959, Joan had needed some time to acclimatise to living at nearly nine thousand feet above sea level, where the air was thinner, but the couple were soon on their way to becoming fully integrated members of Bogotá's elite. As they had thought from the beginning, life consisted of a never-ending round of political and social engagements. Gregorio introduced them to everyone and anyone that mattered.

Adopting a child only enhanced their standing in their community. Pat embraced parenthood and viewed it in much the same way as he did every new assignment. As in his business role, he decided it was important to try and plan for every eventuality, to build a good team and be adaptable. With those principles guiding him, he threw himself into this new role. He had been the driving force behind the adoption and he enjoyed being a father but he knew it would be too much to expect Joan to both play the role of dutiful wife in a foreign land and bring up a child that wasn't hers. He also recognised that the apartment in the Tequendama, while large, was not going to be suitable for a small child. He began looking for a proper family home, one that could be effectively protected. He also hired two maids, Carmen and Otilia, to help Joan and a driver-cum-bodyguard, who would be known to Phillip as señor Martinez, recruited from the Colombian army. He always carried a 9-mm Magnum revolver. Pat was aware of the attention the new cash transfer business was attracting and knew it could spill into his personal life. He enlisted four ex-army soldiers to man a Willys Jeep to follow him wherever he went.

Pat's respectable business executive/family-man persona was only ever designed to be one part of the story of his life in Colombia. After the adoption, he began work in earnest on the secret operation – tracking smuggling gangs. The helicopter raid on the stolen money had been necessary to protect De La Rue's business interests and more work still had to be done to establish the identity of the main players driving the criminal networks. Pat worked closely with his American counterparts, in particular Manuel Noriega – the agent from Panama known as JB. Pat found him ambitious but resourceful and an extremely useful ally. Pat made regular trips to neighbouring Panama, as well as Nicaragua and Costa Rica, to build a network of intelligence contacts in the region. In a volatile environment, however, it was proving difficult to establish trust and build allies.

Arthur Norman, now chairman of De La Rue and a recent recipient of the honour of Commander of the British Empire (CBE), was even keener than before to protect the company. He had made regular trips to Colombia to check on the firm's progress, while keeping Pat informed on dealings back home, where Arthur had almost been as busy as his most trusted agent. Formica, the new plastic Arthur had helped develop, had proved so popular in kitchens the world over that a network of overseas factories was established to satisfy demand. Banknote printing works had been established in other territories and, giving the world its first ATM or cash machine in 1967, the company was developing plans to roll them out to a wider market. It was imperative to avoid cross-contamination with the intelligence work. The little group from London entrusted with Arthur's special project took care not to discuss any details at the offices. They had grown close to their Colombian counterparts, but some things needed to remain inside their circle.

Los Lagartos golf course, in north-central Bogotá, was established as the preferred location for clandestine meetings. The ultra-exclusive private members club was the perfect place to dress up the most sensitive of conversations as a chummy get-together. Such meetings always took place on a Saturday, as Arthur liked to arrive for official business at the firm's headquarters on a Friday with his Colombian partners. This meant that Saturdays would be just another day with the families on parade at the golf club and Pat and his team could meet Arthur without arousing any suspicion.

Pat had newly acquired a black Chevrolet when Arthur was in town for one of these discussions. In a city where murders were so frequent that it often took several days for the police to move the bodies, an armoured, chauffeur-driven vehicle was the safest way to get about Bogotá. Wealthy foreign executives were ideal targets for kidnappers or muggers. Martinez drove Pat to the club, where Arthur had bought along a new arrival.

'Pat, meet Clem Chalk,' Arthur said, introducing him to a shorter, broad-shouldered gentleman with close-cropped hair. 'He's our new accountant and chief procurement officer.'

'Pleasure,' Pat said, shaking Clem's hand and showing his colleagues to the car. 'Welcome to Colombia.'

'Call me Chalky.'

'I've recruited Chalky from our operation in Argentina,' Arthur said.

Pat already had Chalky's roles filled but he knew better than to question Arthur's motives. His boss would explain his reasoning soon enough.

'Business still booming, I see,' Arthur remarked as they drove through the city streets early that morning and passed a body lying next to a dustcart. 'If you're an undertaker.'

'Quite,' Pat said. 'One can never be too careful.'

Arthur nodded. 'What updates do you have for me?'

'Well, Gregorio's swing hasn't improved any,' Pat said. 'I'd rather have young Phillip in a foursome.'

Arthur laughed. The company might be expanding its reach into every corner of the world but the chairman's old-school love of a chuckle at someone else's expense had never left him.

'And what other news?' Pat hesitated. 'It's all right, you can talk in front of Chalky. You will see how useful he will be to you.' He turned to Chalky. 'Show him.'

From his pocket, Chalky produced a small gadget that Pat at first thought was an elaborate cufflink. When he held it in his hand it was practically weightless. 'It's a listening device,' Chalky said. 'We can fit it onto any blazer button. Weighs only four grams.' Pat compared the device to his own jacket button and smiled approvingly. 'And this,' Chalky added, producing a disc no bigger than a shilling coin with a small wire, 'is a bug. Hide it in the room you want to monitor and the receiver will pick up even if you're a couple of streets away.'

Pat inspected it, marvelling at the ingenuity. Arthur beamed. Looking at them both, Pat couldn't help but feel as if he really were James Bond, whose adventures had begun to be turned into movies. If Arthur was M, the intelligence chief in charge of operations, then Chalky was certainly Q, the quartermaster providing the field agent with a range of nifty gadgets.

'Chalky's the man charged with the authority to transfer funds from London,' Arthur said. 'He's my auditor. Handy for putting those more questionable items through the books.'

'Very good,' Pat said. 'Do you have anything in your pocket that locates lost golf balls? If you do, Gregorio will be your friend for life.'

Arthur laughed as if this was the best joke he'd ever heard. There was a serious point. The quip had told the chairman what he needed to hear – that the golf course continued to be a place that their Colombian counterparts did not frequent. His heartfelt laugh was a satisfying validation as far as Pat was concerned.

'I don't have that,' Chalky said. 'But I do have a set of hollow golf balls that are perfect for hiding devices, notes, drugs – you name it.' Pat could tell he was going to get along just fine with the new recruit.

Arthur only tolerated joviality for so long and he quickly turned the conversation back to business. 'How's the young boy?'

'He's doing fine,' Pat said, his heart swelling at the mention of his newly adopted son. 'Quite the character.'

'Good, good. Still no repercussions from that nasty business?'

Pat shook his head. 'All quiet.'

'It won't be for long,' Arthur said. 'And do we know for certain who was really behind that last attack?'

'We have a good idea.'

'From where you thought?'

'It's as you predicted, Gerry – Medellín.'

'Are we any closer to making contact?'

'It's a slow process,' Pat said. 'The gangs there are growing bigger and stronger. JB and Gregorio are using their contacts but we don't have a definitive way in yet.'

'What about the father of the boy?' Arthur's eyes narrowed. 'Is he going to cause us problems?'

'Still no official contact,' Pat said. 'Carlos the banker, the Uribe woman and Gregorio all claim to have links but they are biding their time.'

Arthur nodded. 'We may have to force the issue.'

'How so?' In setting up the business, Pat was content with taking a softly-softly approach. He knew Arthur didn't always have the same patience.

'Just keep an eye on our Colombian friends,' Arthur said, making sure his voice was low enough that the driver wouldn't eavesdrop. 'They will have their own agendas. It's better if we have control. The situation could become volatile – very quickly.'

'Of course,' Pat said. 'We will do all we can but I fear we might have to wait for our friends in Medellín to make the first move.'

Arthur sighed. 'That's what I'm afraid of.'

CHAPTER 5: COLLISION COURSE

Bogotá, 1967

The roar of the approaching motorcycle would have told the figure crouching by the side of the road, scarf wrapped around his head, all he needed to know. As the bike sped past, the rider's thumbs-up was the final confirmation. The armoured car was on its way.

The teenager had been over the procedure a hundred times. He knew exactly what was required. But now, with just seconds to go and the device in his clasp, his hands were shaking so violently he feared he would blow it – and not in the way he was supposed to.

The rumble of the powerful engine stood out from other traffic. It was so loud the boy began to wonder just how big this thing was. The temptation was to stand up, to see with his own eyes that it was real, but he knew very well that this was the opposite of his orders. He was under strict instructions to stay hidden, to do nothing to arouse suspicion. He knew the moment he was waiting for. When the vehicle passed the street sign that would be his cue, his signal to cause mayhem. This attack had been planned to exact revenge. For the lives lost before. For the lost treasure. This was the gang's way of showing these gringos that their criminal organisation should not be messed with. The threat from Medellín was all too real. And this single act was to demonstrate that this boy was ready to do whatever was necessary. That he was ready for the big time.

The rumbling got louder as the shaking got worse. His palms felt as if they were dripping in oil. Surely it should have been on him by now. It was taking its time. He began to worry that the plan had been leaked to De La Rue. There must have been a change of schedule and route. He became convinced that they knew what was about to happen and they were slowing. He might have glanced up, but he was scared to show even a glimpse of his face. And then he saw the armoured car at last. It was passing the sign. Only then did he begin to feel calm. It was all happening in slow motion. Once he made his move there would be no remorse. He pushed the lever down. He braced himself but for a time nothing happened. The armoured car rumbled past. From his crouched position it looked terrifying. A huge metal beast.

Then came the blast. First, the light flash. A short delay and then the bang. The rear end flipped into the air in a dust storm that knocked him off his feet. He lost his senses for a moment, before scrambling to put as much distance between him and the carnage. He half commando-crawled, half staggered until he spotted the gap between the buildings. His escape route. The mess was for others to deal with. He had done his job. Did he dare have a last glance round? He was satisfied. No one was walking away from that.

*

Pat liked to hold his son as he looked out of the eighth floor window of the Tequendama. Sometimes he pointed out landmarks or gave a running commentary on what was happening on the streets below. Often it struck him that the city was like one big living organism, in perpetual motion. He recognised how important that concept was, particularly in his line of work. He had to keep moving. If he stopped, even for a moment, someone might put a target on his back.

Soon he would be moving his little family out of the serviced apartment and into a more suitable home. If the last seven years in Colombia had taught him one thing it was that he could never be too careful. The nature of the business meant that he and the rest of the team were always going to be targets for a number of increasingly sophisticated gangs.

Which was why, as he held his boy up to the window of the apartment one spring morning and looked out over the city below, he was already expecting the call that came.

'It's happened again,' Gregorio said, when he answered the phone.

'I'll be right over.'

Gregorio's face told him everything he needed to know when he arrived at the office. Another one of De La Rue's armoured cars, carrying a significant amount of cash, had been targeted in a roadside attack. 'How many casualties?'

'The entire team. The driver and two guards . . . lost.' Gregorio lowered his head.

Pat nodded. 'Very well. And the truck?'

When Gregorio raised his head again there was a look of bafflement on his face at Pat's response. His colleague seemed remarkably unconcerned by the loss of life. 'It's been blown up.'

Pat shrugged. 'So I understand. But is it a write-off? Can we get it back on the road?'

'I suppose so,' Gregorio hesitated, still looking confused at Pat's priorities in their discussion. 'It's actually in not too bad a state. The injuries sustained inside were from the team not being properly secured. Perhaps avoidable.'

Pat nodded. 'And the cargo?'

'Gone. The truck was completely empty.'

'Good.'

'We've lost the entire team and the shipment and . . . you think that's *good*?'

Pat shook his head. 'A damaged vehicle is unfortunate, but we can always recruit. And with better results next time, hopefully.' Gregorio looked horrified and Pat put him out of his misery. 'It was a set-up, my friend. The drivers know to change routes every time. To fall into a trap by taking the same roads more than once is either desperately unlucky – or it's an inside job. The driver or maybe the whole the team planned to walk away and claim they'd been robbed. The armour protection of the vehicle must have been tampered with to ensure they didn't survive.'

Gregorio looked shocked. 'What are you saying? That you set them up to be murdered?'

'Not at all,' Pat said. 'I had no way of knowing if the vehicle would be targeted but it followed a route it shouldn't have. If they had followed our instructions there would have been no explosion – and the crew would still be here. That they aren't says to me they were the victims of a ruthless inside job. They might not have expected it but they were likely collateral damage.'

Gregorio sighed, shaking his head. 'And the shipment?'

'A decoy. We suspected we had a few weak links in the chain that we needed to expose. Next time the drivers will listen to us when we tell them how to avoid such attacks.'

Gregorio nodded. 'Excellent work.'

Pat shrugged. On this occasion he didn't like being proved right. And if his suspicions about the loyalties of his workforce were accurate, so too, he believed, were his thoughts on the origins of the attack.

'The gang from Medellín,' Gregorio confirmed, when Pat posed the question.

'Maybe it is time to show our hand,' Pat said, thinking of Arthur's words on his recent visit about possible courses of action.

'My thoughts exactly,' Gregorio said.

'OK, it's agreed,' Pat said. 'It's time to speak to Carlos Escobar.'

*

The name Escobar might never have gained its notorious connotations had it not been for a chance discovery nearly fifty years before Pablo was born. A young farmer named Roberto Gavíria was planting bananas in his small plot of land in Frontino, 140 kilometres north-west of Medellín. Legend has it that he stumbled upon a haul of buried treasure: pots filled with jewellery. Deciding not to brag about his discovery, possibly because he feared it would only make him a target for robbers, he discreetly sold the items piece by piece and used the money to start trading in anything he could lay his hands on. That led him to the smuggling business, buying tobacco and alcohol, hiding his stash in coffins and hawking it on the black market. It proved a lucrative business until the day he was arrested. The experience instilled in Roberto a distrust for authority (an instinct that was passed down through his daughter and to her third son, Pablo).

The young Pablo Escobar, like his grandfather, also made his way by making the most out of a situation and had already shown an interest in the black market and a capacity to exploit opportunities. But, unlike Roberto, he wasn't prepared to sit around and wait for an opportunity to come his way. And, again unlike his grandfather, he could not keep his exploits secret. After his daring bank jobs, word soon spread about the bold teenager with ice in his veins who was not afraid to take risks. His reputation grew and the more he was talked about the more he liked it.

Joining a gang in Medellín was easy. There were so many to choose from. Pablo needed a group that matched his ambitions. He heard of one whose members stole cars to strip and sell as parts. To Pablo, that seemed like a lot of hard work for small reward. He had other ideas. Using the cash he had accumulated from his bank robberies, he bribed city council officials to re-register stolen cars. That meant there was no need to break the motors apart and in turn this meant cars could be shifted quicker. Faster turnarounds created greater demand and the gang needed to up their supply of stolen cars. Now, instead of spying an opportunity and pouncing on a car that had been left where it shouldn't have been, Pablo and his cronies got bolder. They attacked people as they sat in their vehicles; they jumped drivers at lights (at a time before car-jacking was even a concept). As he did with the bank jobs, Pablo revelled in the look of fear on the faces of their victims. It was that sense of power again. This only increased as it didn't take long for word to spread about the thefts. Their success sparked copycat hold-ups by rival gangs. Soon all a gang member had to do was approach a vehicle with a gun and the owners would be jumping out of the cars, leaving the engines running. Sometimes they even handed over the keys. 'Here, take it. Just don't hurt me.'

Pablo and Gustavo didn't even need to be armed after a while. The mere suggestion that they were carrying a weapon was enough to encourage their terrified victims, all of whom had heard the stories, to flee. Pablo still wasn't satisfied. He was always looking for ways to expand his operation and quickly recognised that drivers had become scared to stop their cars anywhere, even for a short time, for fear of being robbed. That gave the young criminal an idea. The fear had become real and it could become a commodity, to be traded. What if he could put word out that his gang would protect people from theft – guarantee their car had immunity – for a price? What better way to earn money than sell protection? It worked brilliantly. People were soon paying him and his gang not to rob them. Given his mob were the biggest perpetrators of the crime, it was straightforward to run the racket. He was making money doing nothing. He had cornered both sides of a sinister market.

Given the money that was being made, a criminal with more modest aspirations might have rested on their laurels and waited for the next scam to present itself. Not Pablo

Escobar. Having people owing money inevitably led to some of them being non-payers. And when someone couldn't meet their protection obligations, he wasn't in the business of setting up a debt repayment schedule. Debtors were dealt with severely and quickly. If someone crossed the gang then the gang had to show that person that they would do anything to settle the score. As the wealth accumulated and the gang got bigger it was inevitable that so too did the crimes. Pablo encouraged his gang to send out a signal that they weren't to be messed with. If the debtor wouldn't pay his debts, then maybe his family would – by way of a ransom.

Escobar let the more bloodthirsty of his crew do the dirty work and they seized their first unwitting victim and held him hostage. They called the family who, as Pablo had predicted, were stunned that one of their own could be kidnapped over car protection payments. They duly paid up. For Escobar, it was yet more vindication of his methods and the power they conferred. From car thefts to protection money and now to ransoms, he saw plainly that fear made people bend to his will. The episode broadcast the required message. Suddenly, outstanding 'debts' were quickly repaid and Pablo Escobar was once more restless. If the debtors were all playing ball, maybe it was time to look elsewhere for some kidnap targets.

Such ruthlessness and entrepreneurial nous moved him through the gangster ranks quicker than even he would have anticipated. People were taking an interest in him, not only in his native Medellín but further afield. An intermediary of Carlos Escobar – the lawyer who assisted Pat with the adoption – observed his namesake all the way from Bogotá. He let Pablo Escobar know that his infant son had miraculously survived the gunfight in the hillside village. He also let him know what had happened afterwards, that the boy had been put into care and then adopted by a foreign gentleman. Not all the details were given at that stage.

It was important that Pat and his family were protected but it was also vital to know what the young criminal thought about his son being alive. How would he react? Now Pablo Escobar knew enough to be sure that he need not yet abandon hope of one day being reunited with his first born son.

CHAPTER 6: PHOTO SHOOT TO KILL

Chicó, Bogotá, 1968

My adoptive parents, Pat and Joan, particularly my father, were careful to keep from me the truth of what had happened when I was a baby, the death of my birth mother and what Pat had discovered about my biological father. As far as I was concerned, I had always been called Phillip. I did have a vague memory of being taken to get that teddy bear after I had been adopted. I kept the toy in childhood, but I was blissfully unaware of the murky circumstances around my birth and the first few months of my life.

By 1968 I was walking and talking and becoming a little livewire. To help me burn off some of that energy, my mother Joan often took me shopping with her. There weren't many areas in Bogotá where a European woman could go walking with her child without fear of attracting some unwanted attention, but Chicó was one of them. It might only have been a twenty-minute car journey to the north but it was more rarefied air, even coming from the Tequendama. With its upmarket boutique shops, manicured gardens and wide, clean pavements, it was the perfect place in which to be seen and a regular haunt for Mother and me.

In Chicó, Mother was happy to walk with me by her side but she still took no chances. We never went anywhere without Martinez in his dark uniform, an armed escort. On one of these outings to the shopping mall, the pavement was busy with women buying provisions or simply whiling away the hours before their husbands returned from work. I felt quite the little lad about town in my shorts and braces. We walked along, me holding her hand, taking in the bustle, the colourful clothes, the roar of the traffic and the smell from the street vendors. I loved getting outside and these walks were my first glimpses into the big, wide world beyond my bedroom, a world I'd only really seen from the eighth floor.

Being so young, everything was new and exciting, but even I could tell when the mood suddenly changed. We were outside the shopping centre when Mother's grip tightened slightly. I saw a young man crouch down and brandish a camera directly in front of us. I heard the click of the shutter and he grabbed my arm, trying to wrench me away. Mother pulled me towards him and, for a split second, there was a brief tussle. She held firm. I could hear shouts behind me. The man let go of my arm and fled, Martinez in close pursuit. People around us were still yelling. I looked up at Mother to see her standing, white-faced, hand to her mouth. She moved me over to a fountain outside a clothes shop. I could see Martinez had his revolver out and he was calling out to a group of people. I couldn't see the young man with the camera.

Some passers-by were coming towards us. Others were standing, staring. There were screams from women at the entrance to the shopping centre. I didn't know where to look next and my attention fell on a long rail of clothes being wheeled out of the shop just ahead of us. I was aware of movement behind it and I looked up to see the man with the camera running back towards us out of the shop. I tried to shout, 'Mother!', but the words wouldn't come. There was a clatter as he banged into the rail and stumbled behind the clothes. I heard Martinez shouting behind him before a loud crack made me jump and momentarily silenced all other noise around me as my hearing was swamped by a whistling sound.

Mother pulled me away from the shop but I couldn't help look around. From what I could see of him the man was lying on the ground. People were running towards him, their mouths open wide, but it seemed to me as if no words were coming out. All I could hear was this screeching sound. They were covering the young man with newspapers. Martinez was there, busying himself around the motionless figure. I saw him pick up the man's camera. And I saw a pool of blood seeping out under the newspapers covering the man's head.

'Come on, Phillip.' Mother pulled me with great force and as I heard my name I realised my hearing was returning. Her words were accompanied by the screams and cries and other exclamations from people nearby.

Suddenly, our other armed protection officers surrounded us and we were quickly shown into our waiting car, Martinez joining us. Once safely inside, Mother checked me over, up and down my arms and legs, holding my face and looking into my eyes. Then she hugged me tightly. We made the short journey back to the hotel in near silence. The ringing in my ears stopped but the images would take longer to erase.

Back at the apartment Dad was home earlier than usual. I ran to greet him and he came down to my level. 'You're OK, little chap?'

I nodded and buried my head in his warm embrace.

'That's my boy.' He ruffled my hair and went to make a fuss over my mother, something he didn't always do. 'None of you were hurt, that's the main thing,' he said, before getting up to fix their favourite drinks.

'You think it was . . . ' I heard Mother say.

'Probably,' Dad replied. 'Nothing stays secret for long in this country.'

'It couldn't just have been a coincidence? Someone targeting a western woman with a child?'

Dad shook his head as he handed Mother her scotch and soda. He retrieved something from his jacket pocket. 'Here, look at this.'

I sat up and climbed over to where Mother was sitting. Dad had handed her a photograph. She took one look and gasped. A hand shot to her mouth, just as it had done on the street that morning. I looked over. It was a photo of Mother and me taken outside. In the picture I was wearing my shirt, shorts and braces, the clothes I had put on today. I remembered that the man had taken a photograph before he tried to grab me.

'It was no coincidence,' Dad said. 'He had a specific target. I don't know whether it was a full-blown attempt or whether he was just briefed with taking a photo and got carried away. It doesn't matter.'

'What will it mean?' Mother said.

'No more trips to the shopping centre.'

Dad knew then what else it meant. Now, more than ever, it was vital to move from the hotel. Here, it was too easy to monitor our movements. He stepped up his efforts after that day and soon found a three-bedroom house, built over three levels and located in a middle-class district. The rented accommodation was next door to the home of an army colonel. Dad knew the colonel would have permanent police stationed outside and it would be as safe a place as any. It would only be temporary but that was good. He liked that feeling, for now, at least.

In the short term, I was sad that I could no longer go out for walks with my mother. I was too young to understand the reasons and wondered if it was something I had done. Why was I the one who had to miss out doing something I enjoyed? Being stuck in the apartment meant we had to come up with other ways to amuse ourselves. Joan wasn't what you could call a 'mummy' sort of mother. She left a lot of the day-to-day business of rearing a child to the maids who effectively became nannies. It suited her to take me along when she was doing things she enjoyed, like going to the shopping centre. She was less at ease getting down to my level and playing with me. When we sat in the apartment she liked reading to me – but again it would not be traditional children's stories but magazines she wanted to read. Once she was relaying an article from the *Reader's Digest* about the assassination of President John F. Kennedy and, in particular, how his team kept him alive while they battled to save him. I looked over at the magazine and saw a picture of the president, as many would remember him, smiling and waving, with his wife Jackie by his side.

'Who's that?' I said, pointing to the image of the president.

'Oh, that's Uncle Carlos's friend,' Mother said.

'Which Uncle Carlos?' I had so many. There was the lawyer, the banker and we had other Carloses who dropped by and were all affectionately dubbed 'uncle'.

'Echeverri.' She showed me the picture of the limousine and explained what happened at Dealey Plaza, Dallas, on that sunny day in November five years earlier. 'He and President Kennedy knew each other well.'

Of all my Uncle Carloses, I liked Echeverri the best. He was jolly and fun to be around and he nearly always brought a new toy for me when he came to visit. It was funny to think he knew the president of the United States of America.

Echeverri, it seemed, knew everyone.

CHAPTER 7: UPPING THE STAKES

In Medellín, Pablo Escobar's activities were becoming ever more violent, even before he tracked down the son he had lost to adoption and launched the failed kidnapping attempt. Until that point in his career, his life of crime must have seemed easy. If he wanted someone to do something he either stuck a gun in their face or waved money under their nose. He was finding out that everyone had a price – and a limit.

Now he was experiencing a setback. It seems likely that the same intermediary – the 'friend' of the family who had previously provided crucial information from Bogotá on what had happened to Pablo's son – would have told Escobar that the kidnap attempt had not been successful. He might have told Escobar that it had been a foolish and cack-handed attempt. Maybe a warning was given that he should've known better than to trust people he didn't know – people who said they could get the job done in the capital. It's likely he was told he should have stuck to his principles and employed his own gang, who knew what they were doing. He would have been told that now security would be ramped up around his son. That made the mission to seize the boy doubly difficult.

But when he had time to reflect – not something he was known to do that often – Escobar might have accepted that the kidnap attempt hadn't been a completely wasted exercise. He would now have known where the man from the armoured car company lived, would have known his name was Pat Witcomb and what type of operation he ran. And he would have known that his son was alive. That would have been the most important thing.

'Don't be rash,' his 'friend' might have said. 'It is too soon. Let them come to you.'

Escobar would likely have been sceptical. After all, why would a wealthy foreign man, with power and connections, want to meet him? Surely this man had everything already?

'Trust me. They need you more than you know,' the intermediary would have said. 'Be patient.'

It was never clear who the intermediary was – perhaps a contact of Uncle Carlos Escobar. But, whoever it was, Pablo listened to him, as he mostly did to all friendly advice. But he wouldn't have thought he needed to pay it much heed. Was patience a virtue Escobar ever possessed?

Pat also took the kidnap very seriously and hired a new uniformed guard, taller, broader and older than Martinez. 'This is Señor Barandiga,' he told Phillip. 'He will be your friend. He's always going to be by your side.' What he didn't tell the boy was that Barandiga was a former Colombian military special forces soldier and his own personal bodyguard. Now, everywhere the Witcombs went together, they were joined by the two close protection officers and the Willys Jeep full of armed soldiers.

By this time the family had moved out of the Tequendama Hotel. It had all been done very quickly. Phillip was delighted with his new home. He had a bigger room, more space and it felt more normal for him to be living on a street with his own front door. When he got up in the morning, Barandiga would be down in the kitchen. Whenever he went outside, he was one step ahead. He was big and always professional but had a kind smile and the boy felt completely safe with him and Martinez, who was still their driver. The beefed-up measures were the correct moves to make – for it wouldn't be the last time Phillip's real father tried to take back what he thought was his.

Yet the attempted kidnap in Bogotá was not the only occasion on which everything did not go Pablo Escobar's way. There was one protection racket and ransom victim in Medellín who claimed he had no money. Pablo's gang had gone to his family to ask for the ransom – and they had refused. What now? The man was not important in himself – any value he had was tied to the possibility of him returning home alive. If anything happened to him the gang would never get its money. It was a problem, but not one that Pablo dwelt on for very long.

'Kill him,' he said, when his counsel was sought.

This didn't go down well with gang members. Violence (or its threat) was one thing. Murder would take things to a new level. But this was what Escobar demanded. He saw it as a test of the gang's resolve. If they failed to punish the victim then the world would know their threats were empty. The signal a killing would send out was worth double the ransom on the hapless victim's head.

'Shoot him in the head and dump him at the door of his family,' Escobar ordered. The game had changed. This was the new rule. Cross them at your peril.

For a time, the ruthless addition to the gang's way of extracting money worked beautifully. Debts were paid in record time. But the game changed again. Pablo had long realised he liked raising the stakes. It wasn't long before kidnap victims were killed even after the ransom was paid. Escobar felt it was key to his success to keep increasing the fear factor. Now the word was out. Don't make yourself a kidnap target. You were as good as dead.

Violence begat violence. Rivals began adopting the same tactics, in the same way they had copied the car thefts. People were being killed for money, but sometimes not. Settling a score was good enough reason. Escobar found his name linked to many of the killings, whether he was behind them or not. This is how reputations are forged.

It was not long before the gang's operations expanded on a huge scale. They began to build a lucrative smuggling racket; shipping and selling any contraband they could lay their hands on – booze, cigarettes, appliances, jewellery and clothing. They were making connections beyond Medellín and throughout the Antioquia region, creating loose alliances with other criminal gangs and established smugglers. Their colleagues were doing things differently and were looking into new markets. One, Rafael Puente, smuggled huge shipments from Panama. After being introduced to Escobar at a football match, Puente showed him the art of smuggling – and how to get everyone down the food chain to bend to his will.

Other connections told him about the potential of a drug that was being produced in Colombia from coca paste that was ten times more profitable than marijuana – cocaine. A lucrative trade in the drug was growing. There were opportunities everywhere.

CHAPTER 8: FAMILY MATTERS

Cali, May 1969

It was like nothing I'd ever experienced before. The streets were so busy with people that Martinez had to sound his horn to cut a passage through. Out of my window I marvelled at the huge pyramids of fresh, brightly coloured vegetables on every side, wondering what would happen if someone selected one from the bottom. Everything looked so exotic: even the people looked darker than those I was used to seeing in Bogotá. The smell of grilled meat wafted into the car and alongside the street-vendors were money-changers with their bundles of cash, shouting out the latest rates.

It was my first trip to Cali, a smaller but, it seemed to me, more bustling city to the south-west of the capital. Dad worked here sometimes and my interest had been piqued the minute when, weeks earlier, he came back to announce that the next time he went we would all be going. At such a tender age – and having nothing to compare it to – I had no idea what a normal childhood looked like. I thought every child had armed bodyguards, a security team and a dad who jetted off regularly to foreign countries as well as other cities. But when he explained that the reason we would be going to Cali was to get 'your little sister', even I had the feeling that this wasn't normal.

I might have been confused to hear that we would flying somewhere to get another child but I put that to one side when I knew we would be flying. The commotion beforehand as everyone packed and got organised excited me enormously, almost as much as the anticipation of going on a plane. My only knowledge of flying had come from the model aeroplanes Dad carefully constructed and hung from the ceiling of his study, entwining them as though engaged in aerial combat. Being able to experience the real thing was even more exciting than I imagined. It was only a short flight but that feeling of wonder as we rose above the clouds would never leave me.

We had landed to find a black Chevrolet, identical to the one we drove around in at home, waiting for us. Dad, Mother and I jumped in one, which Martinez drove, with Barandiga and Otilia in a car behind. It was this little convoy that weaved its way through the throngs on the streets. It was getting dark as we reached the hotel and the streets glowed from the light of neon signs. My only real experience of a city at night before then was the new year fireworks display and the bright colours felt they were marking a similar celebration. A green fluorescent 'Camel Cigarettes' sign outside our window was my favourite, but that was not a view shared by my dad. I heard him complain to the concierge that it kept him awake.

In the morning there was time for a quick breakfast before we were on our way again. This time our two cars had an escort. A Jeep crammed with military police officers, like those I usually saw outside our house, joined us and we sailed through the traffic. We only drove for a few minutes before our escort motored ahead to block the street off in front.

'Stay in the car,' Dad said, as our car stopped outside an imposing, official-looking building.

Two soldiers ran to create a small safety cordon around us as Dad and Martinez jumped out and ran inside the building. Even I could sense we were not in the safest part of town and I was happy to stay put as our arrival had attracted a lot of attention from people loitering outside. A matter of moments passed before Dad and Martinez re-emerged, Dad carrying a young girl wrapped in a blanket. I watched out of the window as he carefully handed her over to Otilia in the car behind. No sooner had the two men hurried to get into our car than we sped off.

'Is she OK?' I asked.

'She's very sick,' Dad said. 'She's malnourished. We need to get her to a doctor as soon as we can.'

Suddenly all the excitement gave way to worry as we immediately raced back to the airport. Much of the trip back to Bogotá was made in silence. All I'd seen of the girl was a mop of black hair and she didn't make a sound for the entire journey. As soon as we touched down, we hurried to our waiting transport and sped along with the blue lights and siren of our escort to a hospital. Once there, we were shown into a room and I sat on a chair, bewildered, as a commotion of doctors and nurses surrounded the girl.

'It's touch and go,' Dad said, after the doctors had properly assessed the girl. 'She's more poorly than we thought.'

We spent an uncomfortable night by her bedside. I had no idea who this child was but I felt worried for her and was desperate for her to pull through. The next morning, I awoke to see her with tubes attached to her arm but, to everyone's surprise and relief she was crying – a welcome sign after how unresponsive she'd been. We left her in the hospital to recuperate while we went home for some much-needed rest.

'What's her name?' I asked my mother.

'She doesn't have a name or a birthday,' she said. 'It's up to us to give her a name and choose a birth date for her. We quite like the name Monique.' It was decided her birthday would be 30 November, the same date as that of her adoptive grandmother back in London's Swiss Cottage, whose name was May. The month was May, which seemed to make the gesture all the more apt. The actual year of Monique's birth was harder to determine. My mother thought the girl and I were not far apart in age, even though the girl looked much smaller, which meant she was about four when she joined our little family.

As Monique grew stronger over the next few days, Dad set about transforming his study into a bedroom. After a week he brought the child home and I was finally introduced to my little sister. She was a very sweet girl, reserved and quiet at first, no doubt trying to work out why she had been spirited away from a children's home into our house, where there were so many things she'd clearly never seen before. She didn't say much and any words she did speak were in a local Spanish dialect. At that time, I was becoming bilingual and I spoke more Spanish than English because I spent more time with Otilia and the guards than I did my parents. Monique struggled to communicate but I began speaking to her in Spanish as she slowly recuperated and began having meals with us. Things got a little easier, although Mother struggled, however. She couldn't understand the new child in her care and that hindered her ability to bond with Monique in those first few weeks.

Most of our days as children were spent in the playroom. Monique had never seen toy soldiers before and did not share my vivid imagination so, despite my best efforts, I found it hard to engage her in the full-scale infantry battles I set out on the floor, which often lasted days. Monique did, however, quickly master the art of loading my cannons with old used matchsticks ready to repel the charge of the Light Brigade.

I got my history from a boy's picture book about the great British military blunder at Balaclava, during the Crimean War. It was a gift from my adopted uncle Jack, who lived in Canada and had a cultural role in the Second World War. He had been in charge of ENSA (Entertainments National

Service Association) for Field Marshal Bernard Law Montgomery's Desert Rats. Monique and I became close during my convoluted lessons and she became a little more confident. Soon, she started to follow my lead until our war games had to be put on hold when Dad unexpectedly came home early one night. Seeing him usually meant something interesting was going to happen and, when Otilia hurried us both to the bathroom to get cleaned up, we were even more excited. We emerged to find Dad wasn't alone. He had brought some important people home with him. It was announced that our visitors were from the Banco De Bogotá and, unusually, we would be joining the adults for dinner.

'A very unique treasure has been found,' one of the men told Monique and me in Spanish. 'It is a very special golden raft and your father's company are helping us transport it so everyone will soon be able to see it at the Museo del Oro.' This was the Gold Museum. Looking at my mother in such a way that made it impossible for her to say, 'No,' he then asked me: 'Would you like to come with us after dinner and see it?' It sounded exciting and he added: 'My friend don Gregorio will be there and he has asked that you come. There is someone he would like you to meet.'

My mother nodded. She said Otilia would look after Monique. I think she knew it was pointless to resist when Gregorio got involved.

Villagers discovered a gold raft in a ceramic pot in a small cave in the hills, near Pasca, south of Bogotá and caused huge excitement. The raft depicted the legend of El Dorado, or the Golden One – it was the investiture of a king, covered in gold, going out onto the sacred Lake Guatavita in the Colombian Andes. El Dorado was the name given to the chief of the Muiscas, who was supposed to have covered himself in gold dust and jumped into the lake. He was accompanied by gold offerings and emeralds for the gods. Experts believed the raft dated back as far as 600 CE and it promised to be one of Colombia's most important antiquities.

Accompanied by our entourage of soldiers and guards from De La Rue, we left the house in a cavalcade of vehicles, sirens blazing, to the Gold Museum. We arrived to see a crowd of people outside, along with many photographers and TV cameras. Dozens of soldiers cleared a route for us to pull up right in front of the steps leading to the large entrance. Martinez leapt out and opened my door. I stepped out, bewildered, into a blaze of popping flashbulbs, the soldiers standing to attention. I caught sight of my godfather at the top of the steps. Mother released me and I ran to greet him. Don Gregorio always made a big fuss of me and this occasion was no exception. Another man standing next to him bent down and shook my hand.

'Don Felipe. Good to see you.' He flicked his fingers and a young lady appeared with a large box of chocolates for me to munch my way through. Turning around, he led us through a set of gleaming crystal-clear shining doors into the museum. It was hard to see anything because of all the flashing cameras. With me holding Gregorio's hand, we passed through a large, round doorway, as if we were entering an oversized safe, with a huge door, its hinges measuring some two feet in length.

The man Gregorio introduced to me was the subject of the photographers' interest. He was Misael Pastrana Borrero, a friend of my godfather and the man tipped to become the country's next president. His security team blocked the snappers from the exhibition area and there was muffled whispering as the dimly lit room filled with dignitaries.

A single beam of light pierced the darkness and slowly increased in intensity. It focused on a glass cabinet sat on a waist-high plinth in the middle of the room. This was a magical sight and, easing myself up on tiptoes with my fingers gripping the side of the plinth, I could just about see the object that everyone was discussing with such reverence.

The golden raft was about the size of a large shoe and sparkled so intensely it reminded me of the pictures from my book of bedtime Bible stories, like the one of Jesus receiving the holy spirit after his baptism, minus the dove. I could see the figure of El Dorado surrounded by his entourage, all made of gold. I stared at it in wonder. Then, without warning, the walls started to fill with light. I could make out hundreds of other golden objects in glass cabinets lining the curved wall. One of the men from the bank made a speech and the woman who had given me the chocolates handed out little glass cabinets, about the size of a large shoebox, with replica golden rafts in them. Dad was asked to collect one as a special thank-you for his security services to the Bank of Bogotá. He bent down and whispered in my ear, 'Go on. Go and get it.' Somewhat reluctantly, I stepped forward, but I still have the replica raft to this day – a memento of that incredible night.

The next morning, while playing football with some boys outside in our street, a van pulled up outside the house. Its driver and another man unloaded a television from a trailer. We'd never owned a set. I ran inside where I found, much to my disappointment, that the TV was only staying for the weekend. Dad had hired it so we could watch a programme about the golden raft arriving at the museum. We were going to be on it. By that point though, the excitement had worn off for me. Having already been at the live event, it was hard for me to get worked up about a re-run. Besides, as much as I was desperate for a TV so I could watch cowboy movies, my actual life often seemed more interesting than anything I'd heard about on the small screen.

Everywhere I went I had a fuss made of me. On occasions I sometimes forgot I had a little sister. It seemed no one was in the slightest bit interested in her. It was as if she didn't exist, such was the attention that was on me, this little boy from the orphanage who had no idea of his own story. Monique would be there, but spent her time mainly in the company of the maid and was kept firmly in the background. This was the case in the summer of 1969 when we embarked on our first family holiday. We would be making an extended trip to England and this would be the first time I would see my adopted homeland. I'm not sure if the idea to leave the country was entirely for my benefit or came as a response to the kidnapping attempt at the Chicó shopping centre.

As was becoming customary, there was a hullabaloo at the airport for my send-off. Security closed off the viewing terrace to the general public while my family gathered with various dignitaries I recognised from visits to our house. Gregorio was there with his family and I posed for photographs with the Bautistaes while Dad filmed the event on a V8 cine-camera, before we were whisked through the diplomatic channels straight on to the aircraft.

What was it about me that intrigued people so much? Was it that my dad was so well connected? Or was it something in me? I had no clue then that Pat and Joan were not my real parents. I did, however, suffer from fairly regular nightmares in which I could see a young girl in a red dress. She was clearly hurt and cried out in pain. Every time I woke up after such a vivid and disturbing dream, it was with a keen sense of sadness and loss. I didn't confide in anyone that I had these dreams. I just thought they would go away. But I wondered what they meant.

Having such attention thrust on me, perhaps I should have appreciated that I wanted for nothing. But, being a child, I often wanted what I didn't have and my impatience nearly resulted in me not making that flight. A few weeks before we left, I had decided I needed to break into my pocket money tin. At that time, I collected football stickers and I had realised I would have to wait for an unacceptably long time to fill my album if I relied on swapping stickers with my friends. Instead, I figured it would be better to get Otilia to buy me some more when she did her weekly shopping. All I needed to do was break into the tin and free up some cash. I knew my mother kept a pair of strong scissors in her sewing kit, stored underneath the seat of the telephone unit. I waited for a night when my parents were out to mount a raid.

Monique and I had already been tucked up in bed and I knew I would get into trouble if I were caught sneaking around the house at night, so I needed to be smart. I took off my hard-soled slippers and made sure there were no marbles that could rattle around in my dressing gown pockets. I tiptoed downstairs and heard the sound of Otilia's radio coming from her room at the back of the kitchen as I snuck past and into the lounge. I crouched down and crept across the floor. I slid my hand under the seat lid, found the sewing box and felt around inside for the scissors. Finally, I found them and raced back up to my room without being detected.

What I hadn't accounted for was how much force it would take to break into the tin. I rammed the scissors into the lid a number of times, but to no effect. I decided to make one final attempt, pushing as hard as I could. The point of the blades caught the end of my finger. I yelped in agony as blood gushed out. Abandoning all caution, I ran as fast as I could down the stairs. Otilia jumped to my aid and quickly stemmed the bleeding with a bandage. One of our security officers fetched me a glass of milk to calm me down. Otilia then took me back to bed and stayed with me until I fell asleep.

The interrogation began before breakfast.

'How did you manage to cut your finger? Where did you get the scissors?' I could tell my dad was not happy but he didn't scold me too much. He peeled off the bandage to reveal the end of my finger flapping around, looking as if it would fall off any second. As he made the call for medical assistance I suddenly started to feel weak and shivery. The doctor took my temperature. It was rising steadily and by late evening I was practically unconscious and things were not looking good. Otilia and a nurse came to my room with cold water to cool me down.

I had caught a nasty tropical virus through the gaping wound on my finger. That night, when I was lying very still, must have been a great worry for everyone. By the next morning, however, I had recovered to the point where I was demanding food. Dad came home early that day and brought a radio to my bedside. 'Something very special is happening,' he said. You won't want to miss this.'

All I could make out were American voices coming from the radio, interspersed with bleeps. Then I heard the words that would soon become famous the world over: 'One small step for man, one giant leap for mankind.'

'We've landed on the moon!' Dad said. 'Isn't that amazing?'

I could see the wonder on his face. He sat with me and spent the rest of the evening explaining the significance of the achievement. His enthusiasm was infectious. It sparked in me a lifelong fascination with space and planets but his presence and care also helped lift my spirits. I had to remain in bed for a week but, throughout that time, he sat with me whenever he could. He brought me an *Eagle* lunar module kit model that we built together and we constructed paper aeroplanes. Mine hardly flew and he built little bombers, complete with a hatch, operated with thread – no doubt also acquired from Mother's sewing kit – that actually dropped little paper bombs. Hardly anyone else was allowed to enter my room for fear of contamination and so it was like Dad and I were quarantined together. Whenever Otilia entered with more soup, he rigged up the bomber above the door so I could drop its cargo on her as she entered.

I didn't think it was possible that our bond could grow any stronger but, during those days of self-inflicted bed rest, we grew even closer. My dad might have been this super-connected international businessman with an air of mystery but he loved being a father and mucking about. Maybe breaking the rules as I'd done did have its benefits.

I hadn't realised or been told it at the time but my condition was serious enough for my parents to consider not taking me on holiday. However, after a few days and regular conversations with the doctor, I was deemed well enough to travel. By the time we arrived at the airport I was almost fully recovered. When we boarded the plane, Dad announced that we'd be making a stopover in Miami before we flew to London. When it came to travel plans, Dad often kept certain details from his Colombian friends.

Compared to Bogotá, Florida was extremely hot and humid. As soon as we stepped off the plane the wall of heat hit me. That wasn't the only difference. We had no guards or maids with us and joined the other regular passengers to reclaim our baggage. Once we had negotiated this mayhem and passed through customs, we entered another large hall where an older couple greeted us. This was Aunt Betty and Uncle George, as I was to call them, who lived in Boca Raton, halfway up the eastern coast of the sunshine state. I'd discover many years later that Uncle George was George Williams, the man with the American accent who had met Dad off the plane on his very first flight to Colombia, ten years earlier. Since then Dad and George had become good friends and George and his wife Betty would become my surrogate grandparents as much as they were aunt and uncle. I grew to love them dearly but that first trip was memorable for several reasons.

We spent three weeks in Florida and, during that time, Aunt Betty taught me how to swim in her pool. Walt Disney World had not yet officially opened to the public but, as parts of the park were completed, they had started taking visitors. George and Betty took us for a couple of days in the first week, treating us to a night at the newly opened Polynesian Village Resort.

Despite his accent, George wasn't actually American, as Dad had first thought, but a semi-retired Englishman who had spent many years on a big ranch in Colombia owned by his father. The family sold cattle for beef, but in the main their money came from a leather-tanning business. Betty was an American citizen and after she married George the couple settled in Boca Raton to bring up a family. George had two projects that kept him busy, one of which was helping to run his son's Yamaha motorbike franchise business and the other was acting as an advisor to Arthur Norman, who had been knighted that year for services to British industry.

George had also provided a safe house for us on Harbour Island in Boca Raton, should we ever need to flee Colombia. It was just like my dad to prepare for every eventuality. He'd also made sure the British consulate in Bogotá had granted me a temporary British passport with a visa allowing me indefinite leave to enter the US. I would be able to get to the States as many times as necessary.

I was sad when it came time to leave Florida but my summer of firsts was not yet over. The transatlantic flight was more gruelling than I imagined but better once I discovered that the in-flight movie – *Battle of the Bulge*, projected onto large screens – was on a delay, so if you moved through the cabin, down the classes, you could see it multiple times. As we approached the UK, one of the flight attendants took me to see the captain. I sat on his knee and he let me put my hands on the flight controls.

Landing at Heathrow, the first thing to hit me was the cold. I'd never experienced anything like it. The next impression, after we'd battled through baggage reclaim and customs once more, was the strange black taxis, with their flip-down seats that faced the wrong way. Once we were on our way, London seemed to go on forever. Back home in Bogotá, a twenty-minute ride could get me almost anywhere. The sheer scale of London's buildings and its never-ending rows of houses dwarfed my home city. Eventually, we turned down a delightful little street full of red-bricked Victorian houses that looked like something out of a Dickens story. This was Swiss Cottage and my adopted grandmother's house was in the middle of the tree-lined street.

When May opened the door, I thought I had met the oldest woman in the world. It was an understandable reaction. She was in her nineties, although it was soon clear that she was very mobile and living independently in her ground-floor flat. She was a kind old lady from a very different era who introduced me to cricket and, on the days when she looked after me when my parents were out with Monique, I would keep her updated with the latest scores while she busied herself in the kitchen. I found different ways to amuse myself there, including turning an empty cardboard box into a car, prompting May to call me 'the little boy in the box'. Those days in with May, the long walks together to the local shops, listening to her life stories from the days when homes were lit by gas lamps, were a whole world away from what I knew in Colombia.

Towards the end of our two weeks' stay, we went on a long trip to Edgbaston, Birmingham, a place famous for its cricket. Dad had a car delivered to May's and there was excitement when we heard as we'd be driving along a new motorway called the M1, which had just been extended the year before. The car had a telephone handset in it, like those I'd seen in the armoured cars I had ridden in back home in Colombia. I spent the trip listening to Dad talking to other people via a radio communication system. When I asked what he was doing he said, 'I can direct special armoured car routes for the firm while we're here in England.' He didn't say more and I knew better than to probe. It was getting quite normal for Dad to be involved in something he didn't want to talk about. My mother told me she had given up asking too many questions years before, which was maybe why they worked so well together.

We arrived at a small, two-bedroom flat. This was not the salubrious type of housing we were used to and we were all a bit concerned and disappointed. What on earth was going on? What had happened to our high lifestyle? Mother was certainly not impressed. But this, Dad explained, was going to be our official UK address and we needed it to be able to show we lived in England while Dad applied for my British nationality and residency. He said there had been a mistake with my initial application, which meant the year of my birth would have to be changed from 1965 to 1962. At the time I didn't have a clue what he was talking about. It was many years later before I understood the complexity of his dilemma.

We spent a strange couple of weeks in that gloomy city. Monique and I slept in bunks in one room. One night, Dad crept into the room and quietly placed a large, camel-coloured wallet under my pillow. I woke and was surprised to see him standing there. I found the wallet and muttered my thanks. He patted my head as he whispered in my ear, 'Never tell anyone where you keep all your money.' With that he smiled and slipped back out of the room.

It would be many years later before I appreciated the true significance of the gift – and his very sound advice.

CHAPTER 9: DOUBLE DEALING

Ibagué, Colombia, September 1969

Pat was always in a better frame of mind to talk business after he'd played a game of golf – especially if he won. The Club Campestre, Ibagué, was one of his favourite haunts. The tropical climate, some two hundred kilometres west of Bogotá, was more intense but away from the city and his usual Colombian contacts he didn't feel the heat so much. He and his CIA counterpart, Manuel Noriega, the agent he knew as JB, were confident that no one would be eavesdropping.

'How is business?' Pat inquired when they had changed and were sitting on the terrace, sipping their drinks.

'Booming,' JB laughed.

'For who, exactly?' Pat was always suspicious when he encountered over-confidence.

'For everyone.' JB laughed again.

Pat preferred straight-talking but he'd known this Panamanian long enough to let him have his fun. He had always been aware that his agent friend was working for the CIA, providing intelligence on the latest drug shipments. Noriega had been key to helping De La Rue's armoured car division obtain the right contracts. Now the legitimate cash transportation routes from Colombia through Central America had been established, it would be easy to add a few extra shipments of smuggler cash every now and then, to gain the confidence of the drug gangs. That was the plan at least. However, although they had worked successfully together – most notably on the raid to recover the stolen money – Pat still had his suspicions that JB was double-dealing, manipulative and a self-serving character. Even though they were both in the business of trading intelligence, JB didn't do anything unless he was also compensated financially. Already on the payroll of the CIA, he also expected to be paid by British intelligence – and that meant by Pat – for anything that benefitted De La Rue and, ultimately, the UK's interests in Colombia. Maybe that just went with the territory. After all, JB was providing a service. Shouldn't he be compensated? Probably, but what made Pat uncomfortable was the feeling that JB was looking to make money from everyone he came into contact with – and that included the drug gangs. JB was to introduce him to the heads of these gangs in Colombia and Pat suspected that this would mean another significant contribution being made to JB's private fund. But would he also be paid by the gangs as well? And, if so, where would JB's primary loyalties lie?

In Pat's experience, the best allies were those that had a joint interest in the success of an operation. He believed that his personal relationship with Noriega, close as it might be, might not be enough to secure JB's complete loyalty. The drug gangs benefitted from JB pulling strings, allowing them access into America and they would not want anything upsetting this little arrangement. Pat knew he would have to keep an eye on JB.

'So they are already seeing a return on their investment?' Pat asked of JB's contacts.

'Most definitely.'

'And is the source Pablo Escobar and his gang?'

JB nodded and took a sip of his favourite Scotch. 'It's all happening in Medellín.'

'They're taking advantage of the opportunities presented to them?'

'They certainly are. They are nothing if not ambitious. And quite ruthless.'

Pat didn't need reminding. He might not have had concrete evidence that the incident involving his son was a genuine kidnap attempt rather than someone sending a message or making a bid to get a photo but, even with the added security he had put in place, he wasn't taking anything for granted. And it didn't take much for him to think of the attacks on the armoured cars.

'Can we control them?' he said.

JB shrugged. He took another swig. 'I don't see why not. Control the money and you control —'

'Yes, I know,' Pat said, looking out over the golf course as the sun started to dip over the mountains. 'And we have leverage.'

'Exactly. We always have leverage,' JB said.

Pat agreed. It was important to have the means to apply pressure when required. He made sure that leverage existed in all his foreign assignments, particularly when dealing with those who believed they had nothing to lose. He had to admit to himself, however – never had he known it to be so personal. 'I think it's time to set up a meeting,' he said.

JB nodded and drained his glass. 'With Pablo Escobar?'

Pat took a moment to consider the consequences once again. He'd already given the matter more thought than he ever believed possible. Would he live to regret reaching out to the man who was the natural father of his adopted son? Maybe but, as he always thought, it was better to keep your friends close and your enemies closer.

He nodded. 'Yes, with Pablo.'

CHAPTER 10: THE MEETING

Rural Antioquia, October 1969

It must have sounded like an invading force. The looks on the faces of the villagers and farmers who came out to see the source of the loud rumble heading their way said it all. Pat and his team's presence was being felt long before they arrived.

The leading truck smashed through overhanging foliage and kicked up a cloud of dust as it powered past a series of *fincas* – farms – leading the convoy up into the hills. Two armoured cars, three jeeps, a dozen men and enough firepower to lay waste to even the most spirited militia, or so Pat hoped.

Roaring over dirt tracks so primitive his teeth rattled, he couldn't help but recognise the similarities to their mission of some four years ago. They were once again heading into the unknown with a clear objective and an expectation that it could get messy. As then, he hoped he would end the day being wealthier than he had been when he set out. The difference between this job and the helicopter raid of 1965 was that he wanted to get a signed contract in his pocket, rather than recover stolen loot.

This was a business meeting, Colombian-style. In some cultures, a phalanx of lawyers and advisors were needed as a show of force to assist the negotiating team. In lawless eastern Antioquia, where even the police feared to go, the rules were simpler: meet fire with fire.

'Not far now,' JB shouted, looking up from his map. Pat replied with a thumbs-up.

It was the Panamanian who had set this up, but under what guise was anyone's guess. A coup in his homeland a year previously had seen his key ally, Omar Torrijos, installed as dictator and he had appointed Noriega as the head of military intelligence. Given that JB had already assumed the roles of businessman, diplomat, government official, CIA agent and military officer, the man now wore so many hats it was a wonder he could decide which outfit to put on each morning. Due to his elevated position in Panama he had to spend much his time travelling backwards and forwards but he still liked to get out in the field in Colombia. Pat believed that JB been more or less straight with him to date but, if the Englishman's international operations over the years had taught him anything, it was that stand-up guys were that way only as long as it suited their agenda. The minute Pat's goals wavered from theirs, he was in trouble.

Another factor that Pat was weighing up was the presence of the Colombians. Gregorio and Carlos Escobar were all over this too, but it was a business meeting, after all. This was De La Rue just expanding its operations but, if that was the case, how come they needed so many guns? What had their intermediaries told Pablo Escobar? Pat couldn't be sure. And that gave him concern. They had told him that his connection to Pablo Escobar through his son could only be a bonus in building ties with the gangs. To have an in like this, to access one of the most sophisticated smuggling operations in the region, was a godsend. It was an opportunity to be exploited. He got all that. He asked them what exactly they had told Escobar about the boy. His Colombian friends replied, 'Not a lot,' and he had to assume that meant 'Everything.'

Going by the shopping mall incident in Bogotá, Pablo Escobar must know his name, his address and where he worked. Did he know Roberto's name was now Phillip? Probably. Did he know his routine? Possibly but, with security well-briefed to change routes on a daily basis, he was taking precautions. But what else did Pablo Escobar know? That was what was making Pat uneasy. He liked to go into any negotiations knowing that he had the upper hand, or at least that he had a trick up his sleeve. On this occasion he felt that he was the one exposed.

They rumbled around another bend and the sight of a man with a motorbike at the side of the road, kicking his machine off its stand and hot-tailing it into the distance, signified they were close. Pat gave his men the signal. They cocked their weapons.

The *finca* was at the end of the road, where a track gave way to a small courtyard in front of a two-storey ranch. The motorbike they'd seen only moments earlier lay abandoned outside. Pat clocked figures in all three of the upstairs windows, at the side of the building and, he imagined, waiting to flank his convoy as it entered the yard. He had to hand it to the gang. It was the ideal location. One route in, one route out, vantage points on all sides. They were taking no chances. After the last encounter, the helicopter raid, they obviously wanted to avoid surprises.

The vehicles pulled up and, as Pat instructed, turned to face the way they came. At that moment, five men emerged from the front of the house, each armed with a small pistol or rifle. The armed guards jumped out, their much more sophisticated revolvers and assault rifles ready.

Pat exchanged a look with JB. 'Do we really need all this?'

The Panamanian shrugged. 'Let them have their fun.'

They stepped out of the jeep and walked forward. Pat was dressed like his men, white shirt, black tie tucked in, over suit trousers. He felt slightly incongruous, dressed in a business-like fashion in bandit country, but he needed to underline this was not an attack. Combats and a flak jacket might have suggested he expected trouble. He was armed only with a pen.

The main door was ajar and as Pat took in his surroundings he could make out a figure loitering inside the building. Apart from the odd creak from the trucks there was silence. It was as if even the birds had stopped their chatter to see how this encounter played out. Pat had no appetite for a who-blinks-first standoff and signalled to his men to lower their weapons. They did so but their guns remained cocked. In contrast, the barrels held by the other side remained aimed at head height.

'Amateurs,' JB muttered, in English. Pat smiled.

'Amigos,' he said, this time to the assembled gunmen. '*Relájese.*' The men showed no sign of relaxing. Pat looked up at the *sicarios* (hitmen) at the windows and behind the trucks. He gestured to his men to fall back and stepped forward, his arms open, hoping he was making the internationally recognised sign for, 'OK, you win.'

A large, balding man, one of five at the front of the house, kept his firearm trained on Pat with one hand and held out the other expectantly. '*Tu regalo?*' They had been told beforehand to bring tribute. A sweetener to grease the wheels of negotiations. Pat gestured to one of his men from the armoured cars to step forward. He carried with him a black holdall. Pat took the bag and moved towards the man. Around him the guns twitched. Mindful that some trigger-happy loon might spoil the party, he nevertheless kept moving. He placed the bag at the man's feet and stepped back. The fat man reached down, trying to keep his gun on Pat while simultaneously unzipping the bag. Realising that doing both was a struggle, he tucked the weapon as best he could into his straining waistband and reached again for the bag. Unzipping it, he revealed to the assembled gunmen a bundle of banknotes. Inside the bag was packed more of the same. That prompted some nods of approval.

'*Bueno*?' JB said. The man nodded and chucked the bag to an associate who scuttled inside the door with it. 'Now we can do business, yes?' JB said, addressing everyone in Spanish.

The large man moved to greet him formally, pointing to his chest. 'With me.'

Pat and JB exchanged looks again. Pat smiled. 'No. With don Pablo.'

The man smiled, pointing to himself again. '*Si*. Me.'

JB shook his head. 'I don't think so. The deal was with don Pablo.'

'The deal will be with me.'

'And you are?'

'Big boss man!' He patted the belly his shirt was struggling to contain. The men around him laughed.

Pat's smile remained fixed. 'Funny . . . but, seriously. Don Pablo. We are here to see him.'

The man shook his head. 'He doesn't run this operation.'

'Not yet,' Pat said. 'But he soon will.' He saw some of the *sicarios* exchange glances.

JB approached the large man. 'Enough nonsense. Who can take us to meet don Pablo?'

'I can.' The voice came from the figure standing in the doorway.

'And who are you?' JB said, walking past the larger man. Some of the gunmen didn't know whether to keep their sights on this one, or the tall westerner.

'Gustavo.'

Pat could see this man was younger than the others, tall, almost lanky, but with a fuller moustache.

'He is inside?' JB said.

Gustavo nodded. JB motioned to Pat who was already on his way, Martinez following closely behind.

'Close friend?' Pat said, shaking the young man's hand as they entered the building.

'Family.'

They entered into a large room with a wooden table in the centre. Seated at it were two men. Another couple of guards stood as impassively as statues to the side of them. For a gang of thugs they had assembled an impressive show of force. Pat did a quick scan of the room. The furniture was basic. He doubted the house was lived in and, judging by the location, probably hardly used at all, certainly not as an HQ. He did have one of Chalky's tiny listening devices in the lining of his jacket but he couldn't see there was much point deploying it here. He imagined this crowd would vacate the place before his own dust tracks had even settled.

The older of the two men stood up but offered no handshake. Still more front, Pat suspected. He turned his attention to the other man. He looked younger than everyone else there, including the Gustavo chap, but the beginnings of a moustache suggested he was trying to look more mature. There was a mop of hair that had clearly lost acquaintance with a comb some time ago but there was something familiar about the face; across the eyes especially, which were alert and bright.

Of course, he thought . . . finally.

'Pablo Escobar Gaviria – nice to meet you. I am Patrick Witcomb, of De La Rue, England.'

The young man looked to his colleague for a second, then stood up, puffed his chest out and took the hand that Pat extended. 'And I am Pablo Escobar . . . of Medellín, Colombia.'

He smiled as they shook hands. Pat found his palm warm and clammy but his grip was firm. He pointed to JB. 'My colleague, JB. And you are?' Pat said, addressing the older man.

'Silvio García Rojas. We have a mutual friend.'

There were more handshakes. Pat knew to whom he was referring. 'Uncle' Carlos had worked hard to get them to this point.

'Please sit,' Silvio said. They did, joined by Gustavo.

'I have heard many things about you, don Pablo,' Pat began. 'Your reputation precedes you.'

'And I you,' the young Escobar said. 'For different reasons, perhaps.'

'Quite so. You are aware of what we do,' Pat went on. 'You have certainly taken a keen interest in our armoured cars – and their cargo.' A hint of a smile passed across Escobar's face but quickly vanished. He accepted a roll-up cigarette and a light from Gustavo. He inhaled deeply and his smoke sent a pungent aroma over the table. 'You will know why we are here. We have established our business in Bogotá but, as I'm sure you can understand, we are always looking to expand. We are setting up a new operation in Medellín.'

'You are right. We know,' Silvio said.

'Then you'll know,' Pat continued without missing a beat, 'that we are keen to stop the attacks on our trucks – and to offer your operation our expertise.'

'What would we know anything about any attacks?' Gustavo said.

'Perhaps nothing,' Pat said. 'But we hear you are in the protection business, a bit like us. You might be in a position to influence these matters.'

Pablo remained content to let his relative do the talking but he was clearly concentrating on the exchange. Gustavo said, 'And why would we want to give you our money?'

'As I'm sure our mutual friend explained, this might not seem crucial to your business at this precise moment, but very soon it will. You would be provided with security for transporting money and more. You would receive assistance, not just locally but internationally and, shall we say, politically. We can help with logistical problems and fiscal complications.' Pablo Escobar looked bemused, but Gustavo and Silvio nodded. 'We don't just protect your money, we protect you,' Pat said. 'We have influence everywhere.'

Now Pablo seemed to understand. 'Normally we "influence" things with this,' he said and, laughing, he pulled a pistol from behind his back. Gustavo grinned, leaned across and the two of them high-fived.

They're still just kids, Pat thought. They have a lot to learn. 'Indeed,' he said. 'We know how effective that strategy can be. But sometimes more subtlety is required. Sometimes, all you need is this.'

He reached into his jacket pocket. There was a discernible tension in the room and the gang members, seated and standing, twitched their firearms. Pat produced his fountain pen and placed it on the table. There was a brief pause as though the watching men weren't sure if the pen was going to explode. Then Gustavo laughed. It took another second for Pablo to join him.

'Contracts, agreements, procedures,' said Pat. 'They allow the wheels to turn, obstacles to be overcome. And they cover up a multitude of sins.'

The meeting proceeded. Gustavo had questions about logistics. How exactly would this work? How many armoured cars would they have in Medellín? How readily could they be at their disposal? How could they count on legal, diplomatic or political assistance from their mutual friends? As Pat answered his points one by one, he was impressed by this young man's grasp of the technicalities. He would go far. And yet, fate had decided someone else in his family would be king of this little operation.

Pablo Escobar was reserved. Perhaps he still needed to be convinced of the merits of this arrangement. Yet Pat was in no doubt that he too was taking everything in and studying how he and JB conducted themselves.

After a lengthy discussion, during which Pat thought they were making headway, he and JB took their counterparts outside to inspect the armoured cars, Martinez always a step behind. Escobar peered inside one of the vehicles and appeared impressed by what he saw. He turned to Pat.

'Providing we do this, why should we trust that you will be able to protect anything of ours in one of these? They are easy targets . . . I understand.'

Pat felt his blood temperature rise. 'If you asked the last people to rob us they wouldn't share that view.' As soon as the words left his mouth he felt a tinge of regret. The subject of the raid that killed Escobar's young lover was always going to come up at some point but he had hoped that when that moment came he would handle it with more finesse.

Escobar's eyes narrowed. 'I would do that but you killed them all.'

'Not all,' Pat said, trying to keep a lid on his emotions.

'So I heard.' Escobar was now so close Pat could smell the smoke on his breath. 'How is my son?'

Pat was aware of JB moving closer, though his eyes remained locked with Escobar's.

'He is fine. He is doing very well in fact. He is . . . '

'Mine.'

'And the only reason he is alive is because of me.' Pat lowered his voice, conscious that the *sicarios* were listening. The last thing he wanted was a full-scale argument. Gustavo and Silvio had Escobar's back. One wrong word and it could all kick off. 'You know about his existence because of us. His life is with us now – but one day he will know all about his past.'

Beads of sweat formed on Escobar's brow. The light had dulled from his eyes. His countenance had taken on another complexion. 'His past? His future should be with me.'

Rifles cocked around the truck as the mood darkened. As much as Pat wanted to put this punk in his place he knew his words were crucial if he was to prevent this turning nasty. 'Don Pablo, I salute your passion for your offspring,' Pat said, slightly bowing his head, his tone softening. 'It is admirable. It has never been my intention to deny this boy his heritage. It is right that he should know about his father.'

Going by the continuing blank look on Escobar's face, Pat wasn't sure if that was enough to satisfy him.

'How about you get to meet the boy?' Gustavo said, placing a hand on his relative's shoulder. 'What do you think, Pablo? You get to see he's all right, you can say, "Hello," – we take it from there?'

Pat looked to JB who shrugged as if to say, it's your call. He then nodded to Gustavo. 'That could be arranged. Of course.'

Escobar nodded. 'Yes, I want to meet my boy.'

Gustavo patted him on the back. 'Nice one, cousin. We move forward.' The tension began to lift. They stood and discussed potential future meetings, establishing points of contact. As the visitors prepared to leave, Escobar shook Pat's hand and thanked him for making the journey and for agreeing to their various demands.

'Tell me, señor,' the young Colombian stared into Pat's eyes, 'when you flew in the helicopters and you killed everybody, including even innocent victims, was that all really necessary?'

'We had to take back what was ours,' Pat said calmly. 'We would do the same again.'

'Well then,' Escobar said in a low voice, 'you won't be surprised when I do the same.'

CHAPTER 11: YOU ARE AN ESCOBAR

Medellín, New Year's Eve, 1969

As soon as I saw them, I got the feeling they were different. They didn't look like us. They didn't dress like us. They didn't behave like us. I could tell these men were rough.

What made it more incongruous were our surroundings. We were in one of the city's swankiest hotels. Massive crystal chandeliers loomed over dozens of round tables, each of which seated at ten people. A stage that traversed the whole of one end of the ballroom suggested there would be entertainment at some point in the evening. For now, though, it was a bit of a free-for-all. There were lots of kids running around, many of whom I knew, as they were the children of those friends of Dad's who visited the house or his various clubs and those I'd met at the embassy parties our parents dragged us along to while they were socialising. I wasn't allowed to run around that night, however. I had been told to sit tight for the time being, Barandiga and Martinez close by me. I felt hard done by – that I was missing out. But I did as I was told. The way the bodyguards' hands hovered over their holsters told me this wasn't like our usual get-togethers.

For a start we were in Medellín, the second city of Colombia and a place that to me had neither the status of Bogotá nor the charm of Cali. From the moment we'd stepped off the plane the atmosphere had felt gritty and, even though we were here to celebrate the dawn of a new year, there was a detectable seriousness about the proceedings.

Our table was near the stage to one side. My parents and their friends were suitably attired in their finery, befitting our surroundings but it was one of the men who occupied the other tables in our area who really held my attention. He wasn't the tallest – and certainly wasn't the oldest – but there was just something about him.

Dad was in business mode, I could tell. This might have been a family event, but I could tell he wasn't relaxed. Even when he was talking to someone he was scanning the room, alert to any eventuality. In fact, everyone seemed a little tense, like they didn't really want to be there, which I thought was odd as, to any observer, it would have seemed like a big party.

I began following my dad's gaze. His concentration was focused on the men near us and, in particular, the man I'd singled out. What was it about this man? He didn't look like my Carlos uncles – either the banker or the lawyer – or like Gregorio. He didn't look particularly smart. His shirt was loose-fitting, casual and open-necked. Whenever he stood up I could see he had a bit of a paunch and his trousers, held up by a belt, were baggy, creased and in desperate need of a pressing, not like my dad's, which had one neat fold the length of his leg. His hair was untidy and its grease shone under the ballroom lights. Yet people kept coming up to him and leaning over the table to get a word. I couldn't help but stare. Then his eyes locked with mine. I was used to people looking at me curiously but this was different. I'd never had someone look so intently at me. I had to look away, suddenly feeling self-conscious. One of the men who had been speaking with him got up and approached our table. Dad stood up and greeted him with a firm handshake. The man was looking down at me. Over at the table the younger man kept staring too.

'Phillip,' my dad said, 'Can you come here, please?'

I stood up, grateful to be by my dad's side.

'This is don Silvio. A business associate of mine,' he said, in Spanish. The man half-smiled and nodded a greeting. 'He would like you to meet someone. A friend of his.' Somehow, I knew exactly which man this friend was going to be. I started to feel strange and looked up at Dad for reassurance. 'It's perfectly fine,' Dad said, smiling as he placed a hand on my shoulder. That made me feel better.

'This way,' the man said, taking my hand and showing me across to the table I'd been staring at. As we crossed the hall, people started to move out of the way to let us through. Someone sitting right next to the man I'd been looking at earlier hastily jumped to his feet and offered me his seat. The man pushed his chair back to create a bit of room. Silvio said something and stepped back. I looked across at Dad, who was watching only a few feet away. He smiled and nodded. Barandiga was now standing by his side. I edged closer and got a whiff of cigarette smoke mixed with pungent musky cologne. Something stopped me from sitting down.

The man sat back and considered me. He had a thin moustache and, when he smiled, he revealed a row of yellow teeth.

'Don Roberto.' His tone was deep, gruff and semi-formal.

I must have looked confused. Silvio leaned forward and whispered something.

'Ah, don Felipe!' the man said. '*Siéntese, por favor.*' I did as he asked and sat down, but perched at the very edge of the chair. The man leaned in and said muttered something so quietly I couldn't quite catch with all the noise around from the surrounding tables. I was also keeping an eye on the men next to him. They were more excitable and were mucking about and making a big deal about drinking lots of liquor. I caught a glint of steel at the waistband of the man next to me and I suspected the others were all carrying something too. At the mention of the word '*padre*' – 'father'

– though, I again tuned into what the man was saying and looked across at Dad. The man laughed and followed my gaze. He asked me what I liked doing, if I liked football.

The man spoke so quietly I wasn't sure if he was trying to make sure the men beside him couldn't hear. I just shrugged. It was a strange feeling. The other men made me nervous but I felt like this man wanted me to like him. I didn't feel threatened by him. We only sat like this for a few moments and, throughout that time, I stayed silent, only smiling when I thought I could make out something he said. I just knew that in situations like this, when I was mingling with adult associates of my dad, I had to be on my best behaviour. After a few minutes more I saw Dad look to Silvio and, as if in response, he leaned in and whispered something to the man. The man sat back in his chair once again.

'Adiós, mi hijo,' he said – 'Goodbye, my son' – now at a volume I could understand. 'I will see you again. And always remember little man – you are an Escobar.'

Dad approached and gestured to me to join him back at our table. I did so.

'I have to hand it to you,' the man said to Dad in Spanish, 'The choice of venue and the location? Inspired. In the open, in front of so many people here to celebrate. The perfect cover.'

Dad smiled but he put a firm hand on my shoulder. 'It was so everyone could be here. We don't want anyone to feel left out.

'I have to hand it to you, gringo. You have been true to your word,' the man said.

Dad pulled me closer into him.

'And I will be true to mine,' the man added, laughing.

I saw Dad offer a thin smile and he led me back to our table. 'Who was that man?' I said.

'Just someone we're going to be doing business with.' He smiled and said I could sit down again. The rest of the party passed by in a blur. There was music and dancing and, when midnight came, loud cheers and banging from outside. The festivities didn't excite me as much as the fireworks I had seen in our home city, however. When it was time for us to leave I was so tired I struggled to stay awake. I caught one last glimpse of the man who'd taken such an interest in me. He was standing looking at me. There was something weirdly familiar, yet also strangely alien about him.

CHAPTER 12: THE BIG GAMBLE

Pat had spent quite some time weighing up the risks of introducing Phillip to his biological father. He wouldn't have called them second thoughts. It was more like a continual, dynamic risk assessment, of the kind he carried out every day of the week. He played out different scenarios, assessed the outcomes. The reward had to outweigh the risk. And there was no denying the reward here was huge.

Keep Pablo Escobar on side – and with him the main smuggling operation in Medellín – and Operation Durazno could get into full swing. There would be no more playing catch up. De La Rue would be on the front line with the cocaine traffickers. They would be able to track the money. They would be able to provide the US with the intelligence it desired so much. They would achieve the goals set out by Sir Arthur all those years earlier. They would be able to lessen the risk of attacks on the armoured cars. They would have influence in an area that had so far been out of their reach. Pat could manoeuvre De La Rue into a win-win situation.

The downside was equally clear. Pat might be putting his only son in grave, mortal danger. It didn't matter how many times Pat weighed up the options, that one factor always seemed to tip the scales. And that was almost enough to make him walk away from the whole deal. Ever since he'd set eyes on the baby in that bullet-riddled house he'd felt an overwhelming urge to protect him. Back when he was a young man working for the police, he had harboured dreams of becoming a father one day. When he looked back on those days he had to laugh, of course. Naively, he had thought he could map out a life for Joan and him. He never could have imagined the path he'd go down once he left the force. He might have travelled the world and been involved in work the average person wouldn't be able to comprehend but some things had remained constant – that feeling of wanting life to mean something, to have a family with which to share it all. When they hadn't been able to conceive he'd feared he might have to park those dreams. Then fate delivered him a son. This was how he had viewed that little boy, almost from the moment their eyes met. Pat had needed the baby as much as the helpless tot himself needed a father. For the last four years he had doted on him, taking him everywhere he could, trying to fill his life with as many rich experiences as he could think of, even giving him a glimpse into his own world, one the boy couldn't possibly understand – at least not, for a long time.

And now was he risking jeopardising all of that? Or was he perhaps just doing the best he could? He wouldn't do this lightly. How it played out from here was anyone's guess. But he would do all he could to minimise the risks. He'd already tried to think of everything – armed bodyguards, a passport and visa, a safe house. If the worst happened he'd take Phillip out of the country if such a move were necessary to keep him safe.

There was another thought he couldn't shake. He couldn't deny the boy his past. Phillip would have to learn the truth one day. And he would be able to tell him how he had contact with his real father and the role he played in one of the most ambitious intelligence operations ever achieved on foreign soil.

First, though, he had to try and convince Pablo Escobar, the young criminal with the already fearsome reputation, that he was here to help him. He'd worked with every kind of crook and hard-nut and his job had never been this personal before.

CHAPTER 13: KNIFE-EDGE

Bogotá, July 1970

I was still a young boy but to me it was exciting and thrilling, if a little scary. The sound of gunfire and explosions reverberated across the city. Our house, like the rest of Bogotá, was in lockdown. We were all ordered to stay indoors but I was so captivated by what was going on outside I crept out onto our balcony to watch the drama unfold. I couldn't believe my eyes. A tank rumbled down the street, flanked by men with guns. What was going on? I cowered back behind the balustrade, terrified of what might happen, should one of the soldiers catch me looking.

Inside, Dad either paced the floor or was on the phone. His security team was guarding us day and night while the citywide curfew was in place. We normally only had one armed security officer outside the house at any time but now the house was surrounded by a team armed with machine guns as well as their regular 9-mm revolvers. We even had one chap sitting in the entrance corridor. He looked so miserable stuck there in a confined space that I took him things to eat and drink, in return for some morsels of information about what was happening out on the streets.

Ever since the events of April 1970, the country had been on a knife-edge. That was the date of the presidential election and it was momentous for many reasons. It was the first occasion on which the president and parliament's two houses, the Senate and the Chamber of Representatives, were elected on the same day. For the presidency, Misael Pastrana, Gregorio's good friend, was the Conservative candidate, up against Colombia's former military dictator, Gustavo Rojas Pinilla. At the time the Liberals and the Conservatives had formed an alliance called the National Front to prevent Rojas establishing another dictatorship. Their pact meant the presidency alternated between the parties, with only Conservatives allowed to stand in 1970.

Rojas had formed the National Popular Alliance party (ANAPO) with his daughter María Eugenia Rojas Correa and ran a populist campaign that went down particularly well in the rural communities. Rojas appeared to be ahead in the voting until communication systems malfunctioned nationwide. By the time the system was restored, votes had been counted. Outgoing president Carlos Lleras Restrepo declared Pastrana the new premier. However, he won by a margin of less than one per cent of the vote, sparking claims of electoral fraud by Rojas and his supporters. Amid a storm of controversy, Restrepo stuck to his guns and insisted Pastrana was the president-elect. The ANAPO party challenged the result and the case went before the electoral court. On 15 July it ruled in favour of Pastrana, prompting widespread protests as Rojas called for public demonstrations and the army was mobilised to quell the uprising. Throughout Bogotá and other flash points across the country, violent clashes broke out between protestors and government forces.

It was strange to think that the man I had met a year earlier was now president and battling to restore order in a volatile nation. The military lockdown had paralysed the country and De La Rue suspended the armoured car cash transportation business, while the security officers, who would normally be manning the trucks, were diverted to close protection duties. Despite the disruption, which Dad was hopeful would be only temporary, Pastrana's success had shown the influence of De La Rue and its Colombian partners.

By 1970, Thomas De La Rue had gained a foothold in several South and Central American countries, including Panama. Don Gregorio was one of Pastrana's principal backers and, as I'd witnessed on that special night at the museum, the two men had become close allies. Before the election campaign began, both were regular visitors to our house. Pastrana's immaculate pinstripe suits always carried the smell of cigar smoke. Whenever he saw me, Pastrana would place his hands around my face and say, 'Ah, *mi amigo*, don Felipe.' I enjoyed the attention but had no idea why I was the recipient of such adulation.

My godfather Gregorio had long held a vision of his friend becoming president one day which would secure his own position and turbo-charge his ascendency through the ranks of the country's business elite. Pastrana had used the vast donations pouring in via De La Rue to mount his successful bid for the presidency. Now he was in office, yet no one could have dreamed it would be so difficult. My parents had never experienced anything like this in their time in Colombia. With each passing day it felt increasingly like a military coup might be underway. The mood in the house was sombre as we tried to tough it out but, as the civil unrest stretched on, my parents were forced to leave when Monique fell ill.

Monique had still been recovering from the effects of the malnutrition she had suffered as an orphan and she still needed regular hospital attention. On the day she suffered her relapse and was admitted to a clinic, my parents announced they were going to be leaving the house to be with her, taking the team of security guards with them.

'Don't worry, we'll be back by 6 p.m.,' Dad said.

Otilia was charged with looking after me and we had Barandiga for protection. Given the situation outside, however, we felt more than a little vulnerable. As the house fell silent, I took up my usual hiding place behind the curtains and listened to what sounded like a war outside the window. Six o'clock came and went with no sign of my parents or the security team and Otilia started to get anxious. She pulled me close to her on the sofa. She was trying to hide how scared she was but I could taste salty tears as she cuddled me. This made me feel worse. What did she know? Why was she upset? What had happened to them?

A loud bang on the door made us both jump. It was a sound we weren't used to as there was normally a security guard out front.

'Go hide,' Otilia ordered as she went to investigate. I didn't need to be told twice and scurried back behind the curtain.

She'd just left the room when there was an almighty boom outside. Was that a tank round? It felt like the end of days. I tried to remain still but I was trembling so much the curtain shook. I could hear someone opening the door but then there was silence and as I imagined all the horrors that could be happening downstairs I wet myself. I was almost too scared to move but, oddly, I became preoccupied with the trouble I'd be in for making a mess and for being out of bed. Somehow, I got an urge to bolt from my hiding place. I scrambled up the stairs and jumped into bed, hiding under the sheets, praying I would wake up in a minute to discover it had all been a horrific nightmare. Then I heard footsteps coming slowly up the stairs.

This was no dream. I was not imagining things. Someone was in the house and getting close. It sounded like someone trying to tread carefully. Surely, Otilia would not do that? And if it wasn't Otilia or one of the guards, then who could it be?

The footsteps became louder as whoever it was advanced up the wooden stairs to the landing outside my room. My whole body was now juddering with terror. Tears ran down my cheeks but I was too frightened to sob or scream. I had no power to stop whatever was coming for me. I was completely defenceless. Outside were still the sounds of gunfire in the streets. We were under attack from all sides. I trembled under the sheets as my bedroom door slowly opened.

'There you are. I wondered where you were hiding.'

The relief I felt at seeing Otilia was indescribable. I jumped out of bed into her arms. 'Who was it?'

'It was no one,' she said, noticing my little accident and going to get clean pyjamas. 'Barandiga had a look but there was no one there. Must have been pranksters. Just trying to scare us.'

Finally, I could exhale. It felt like I'd been holding my breath for half an hour. 'And Mum and Dad?'

'I don't know where they could be, little one. Maybe they have been held up at the clinic or they are waiting for the all clear before they come home. I'm sure they won't be long. It sounds worse than it is outside.'

I fell into her warm embrace. As the adrenalin wore off I suddenly felt exhausted and desperate for my bed. Otilia tucked me in and I was overcome with a desire for sleep. I started to doze off almost as soon as my head touched the pillow. I was aware of her talking to me. Perhaps she was reading me a story just to send me off. All thoughts of being scared drifted away. I was vaguely aware of a presence at the door beyond Otilia and felt sure it was Dad, back from the hospital. I felt I needed to speak to him, opened my eyes and, through my drowsy haze, I tried to focus so I could hear what took them so long. I could just make out he was holding something in his hand and, when I rubbed my eyes for a better look, I was shocked to see it was a gun. What was Dad doing carrying his gun in the house? Why was something obscuring his face? It was a mask of some sort. Why would Dad be wearing a mask? Then it clicked. It wasn't Dad!

I pushed back the sheets and wriggled to sit up and see past Otilia as my eyes fully focused. It wasn't a mask. It was a bandage wrapped around his head. I screamed. Otilia turned. Her hand went to her mouth and she instinctively put her body between the intruder and me.

The man shouted, 'Get up! Both of you. You're coming with me.' His voice was muffled through the gauze. I could just make out two dark, wildly staring eyes.

'No!' Otilia tried to protect me but he jabbed the gun into her face.

'Move!' the man yelled.

Otilia stood and I scrambled out of bed, shaking with fear once more. Even if I'd wanted to speak I couldn't find the words. She scooped me up and I buried my face into her neck. The gunman ushered us out of the room and towards the stairs. How had he managed to get past our security? Where was everyone? I don't know whether Otilia was stalling for time or if she was just so terrified that every step required supreme effort but we inched along to the stairs.

'Down. Go!'

Gingerly, she took each step, all the time whispering in my ear: 'Don't worry. Help will be here soon. I will not let him hurt you.' I turned my head to see we were almost at the foot of the stairs. From there it was a short walk to the front door. We would be out in the street – and then what? I was vaguely aware of blasts echoing across the city. In the confusion and with a curfew in place, who would notice a woman and child being bundled into a vehicle on a residential street? Would I ever see my family again?

I turned the other way and looked right into those dead eyes. I could scarcely bring myself to take in the grotesque figure but I could see the bandages were grotty and threadbare. His shirt and jeans were grubby, and he had worn trainers on his feet. His whole demeanour screamed desperation more than it did seasoned kidnapper. I then saw the pistol still aimed at Otilia's back. Every hesitation prompted a jab of the barrel.

'Hurry! Move!' The shouts kept coming through the bandages.

We reached the bottom of the stairs and he pushed Otilia so violently she staggered forward and, for a moment, I thought we were going to fall forwards. I gripped on to her as she somehow regained her balance.

'We are moving,' she yelled. I could hear some anger seeping into her voice.

BANG! The blast was so loud I thought my eardrums had shattered. Otilia gasped and pulled me down to the floor, pulling me tight to her chest.

'You're OK.' The sound around me was muffled by the ringing in my ears, but even so I could make out Barandiga's voice. I could also make out someone crying and I realised it was Otilia. Her grip on me relaxed and I looked around. My bodyguard was standing over us, gun drawn. Behind us on the floor lay the prone body of the gunman, his legs twitching, a pool of blood seeping on the floor under his chest.

'You're OK? You're not hurt?' Barandiga came down to our level. His voice was barely audible but his tone was soft and reassuring. Otilia stood me in front of her and they both checked me over.

'I'm OK,' I tried to say, although I could hardly hear my own voice. The ringing in my ears was as it had been after the gun was fired on that day in Chicó, only Barandiga's shot had been so much nearer and a hundred times louder. Otilia picked me up once more and took me back upstairs to my bedroom. I was fully under the covers but freezing cold; it was as if ice had replaced the blood in my veins. My body wouldn't stop shaking.

'Where's Dad? Where are they?' I kept saying over and over.

'They'll be home soon, don't worry,' Otilia said, more in hope than expectation, I suspected.

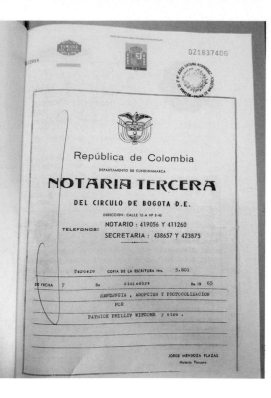

Cover of the author's adoption papers, dated 7th December 1965.

The author's adoption certificate. Unusually, this shows that the adoption was sanctioned by four government ministers:

The governor of the province of Cundinamarca.

The secretary general of the province of Cundinamarca.

The foreign secretary of Colombia.

The official stamp of the British embassy of Colombia.

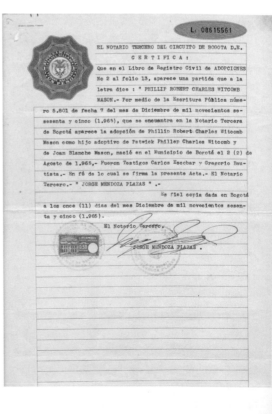

The author photographed by Joan Witcomb, walking outside the 'Chico shopping centre' Bogota, 1968.

The author at the military riding school of Surala, with Achilles, a gift from Misael Pastrana Borrero, President of Colombia.

The author, outside the house of a Colombian army colonel his dad was visiting. He was left outside with the guards who took this picture with the driver's cap on, 1972.

De La Rue guards offloading black sacks of cash at Bogota airport. The same sacks of cash the author witnessed being handed to them at the beginning of the trip on the tarmac at Medellin airport.

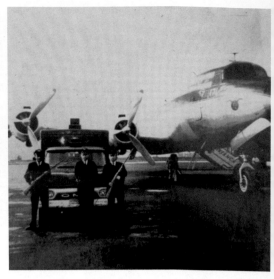

De La Rue guards. The author recalls the trip in this old plane. Even at a time when there were Avianca Jets sometimes Patrick Witcomb would use this old thing to be more discrete when handling cash from Medellin.

The author revisiting the headquarters of the firm in Colombia during school holidays, 1974. The armoured car that used to take him on the school run not so many years earlier. The author is standing with his chauffeur, Mr Martines, *(left)*, and bodyguard, Mr Barrandiga, *(right)*.

A visit by HRH Princess Anne to Colombia, 1973. Present in the picture:
Sir Arthur Norman, chairman of De La Rue *(top left back)*
Sir Peter Barma, managing director of De La Rue UK *(centre back)*
Don Gregorio Bautista, chairman of De La Rue Colombia
Patrick Witcomb, managing director De La Rue Colombia

Don Gregorio Bautista, with his wife and children pictured with the author, in a poncho, Bogota airport 1969.

The author with Joan Witcomb and Patrick Witcomb, Bogota 1968.

Patrick Witcomb with Hernando Bermudes, revealed by the author's dad as his counterpart in the Colombian intelligence services.

The author with "Don Silvio" *(alias)*, 1967, on one of what would be many trips by helicopter to the finca in Medellin.

Author's dad and a four-man security team, on the road to Hirardor Colombia.

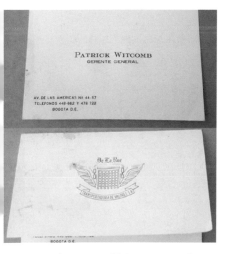

Patrick Witcomb's business card.

Patrick Witcomb *(left)* with Clem Chalk ("Chalkie")
the quartermaster *(centre)*.

The author would phone his parents in Colombia from this phone booth, a minute's walk outside the grounds of Lucton School in Herefordshire.

The author and his dad outside his grandmother's house in Swiss Cottage London, 1977.

🔑13-3-NINE🔪1.17°3°.-2

The author and his dad, Costa del Sol, 1989.

The ringing in my ears subsided and I could make out noises downstairs. The voices of a large group chattered in very excited tones but, amid the Spanish – such a tumult of loud discussion that I couldn't clearly make out what was being said – the pattern of one voice alone stood out. And it was the one I'd never been so relieved to hear. Dad was back with his team and he was demanding to know what had been happening. I could hear him speaking to Barandiga, no doubt getting a debrief of the evening's drama. Moments later he was at my door – it was really Dad, this time. He came in and sat down, cuddling me tightly.

'I'm sorry this happened. It shouldn't have. Are you OK?'

He saw how much I was shaking and picked me up and carried me downstairs where Otilia fixed me a warm drink and something to eat. The body of the gunman had been removed.

Dad explained what had happened. One of our security guards was attacked when he answered the door. By the time Barandiga, who was inside, realised there was a problem, the intruder was already heading up the stairs. Rather than spook him, running the risk that he would believe he was cornered and indiscriminately open fire, Barandiga gambled that the gunman would try to kidnap me and get me out of the house. He knew he would get a clear shot at the intruder before he reached the door. I wanted to see for myself that the criminal was gone. Dad led me down to the hallway. A streak of blood across the stone floor was the only remaining evidence of the terror that had visited our home. Soon even that last trace would be cleaned up.

My mother had been spared the trauma, having elected to stay with Monique in the clinic. Dad was determined that she remain in a state of ignorance over the events. 'Not a word to your mum,' he said, as he led me back to my room. 'She'll only panic and want to move us all back to England. It will be our little secret, OK?'

I nodded, just grateful to have him back with me again.

'I will never let anyone hurt you,' he soothed. 'You are such a precious little boy. And I will do everything I can to protect you.'

I got back into bed once more and, eventually, I drifted off, but the events of that night would haunt my already tormented dreams for years to come. I was still so young but even then I couldn't escape the feeling that trauma, violence and death seemed to be stalking me. How long would it be before they visited me again?

CHAPTER 14: WHO TO TRUST?

Pat was furious. Someone had breached his security and managed to get into his home. He demanded answers from his De La Rue associates, Gregorio and Echeverri, and from Carlos Escobar, who had provided the links to the gang in Medellín, and also of JB. Someone must know something.

The denials were as strenuous as they were expected. No one likes being associated with failure and there was no admission from anyone in Medellín of involvement in the kidnap attempt. Why would they arrange such a thing? Pat's Colombian counterparts told him that it made no sense for them to double-cross him at the very time when trust and cooperation were what both sides were striving for. Was it not more likely that the home invasion was a manifestation of the protests and the anarchy on the streets? It had been a coincidence. It was surely just another example of the president's allies being targeted, an illustration of how he could not even protect the friends who had helped put him in power. The bandages the intruder wore were evidence that he was not connected to the gang in Medellín. Many of the protesters donned similar makeshift hoods to avoid detection during the demonstrations. Pat was left to ask himself if it was really credible to suggest that a criminal gang had not tasked the gunman. Was it really only coincidence, or bad luck, that one lone protestor decided to mount a solo raid on a guarded house with the very specific goal of kidnap in mind?

Pat's gut told him that Pablo Escobar was behind the night's raid. It was proof that the young gangster could not be trusted. Even if this were true, his Colombian friends said, without solid evidence it was unwise to start attributing blame when both sides were trying to build trust. Amid the chaos Pat had to admit he no option but to carry on. The dust settled but in the course of doing so, it covered everything.

The unrest continued and Pat felt uneasy about his Colombian friends, but at least his son was safe. That was good. It was a terrible thing to happen but there were greater issues at stake. Gregorio's great plan now seemed to be hanging in the balance as Pastrana battled to keep control. They couldn't predict everything that was going to happen. It was the nature of the peculiar business they had entered into. If Operation Durazno was to succeed it didn't pay to dwell on these incidents. There was a bigger picture to think of.

Pat could imagine that Pablo Escobar was also thinking of the bigger picture over in Medellín, where there had not been the same widespread lockdown as the capital had experienced. He would have figured, if it had indeed been a genuine kidnap attempt, that it was worth taking what was after all a free shot. Pat imagined that Escobar was like any criminal, whether a low-level crook or an organised gangster. He would never let an opportunity go to waste. The ongoing political situation had provided that opportunity. While people were already fighting fires, that was the time to throw a bomb, surely?

He wondered, would Pablo Escobar care if Pat suspected he was behind the kidnap attempt? Probably not. Did he even want custody of the boy? Pat didn't know. He could imagine it was purely a matter of pride. What man liked to think that a foreigner was raising his first born child? That his boy should be calling Pat 'Dad' and was growing up believing some gringo was his father? Pat could understand that must be galling. But raise the boy? That was another matter. What would Escobar do with a young child? Probably farm him out to his mother, sister or aunt. Pat suspected that Escobar and his cronies had other problems to worry about, besides the fate of a young boy.

The curfew had suspended business. The unrest had affected the influence that foreign companies had on the economy. Pat could imagine Escobar and his ilk crowing, delighted that the rich foreigners were now finding out that it was one thing to have an ally in the Casa de Nariño – the presidential palace – but it meant nothing if the president was a lame duck. Unless Pastrana could get a grip on the country then, gang relations aside, it was going to be a difficult period for De La Rue. If nothing else, it would be interesting to see how the changed situation was going to affect their new friends. Rojas had called for a people's army to rise up to fight what they felt was the injustice of the presidential election of 19 April. Now a guerrilla group was forming, calling itself the 19th of April Movement, or M-19. Pat couldn't imagine that joining up or working with political revolutionaries would hold much attraction for drug-smugglers but he could not be too sure. The rise of M-19 could have significant implications for everyone – not just the politicians.

Pablo Escobar had shown himself to be an astute criminal. Pat wondered how much attention he paid to politics. Most young people he had encountered since arriving in Colombia took the view that politics was all about keeping the wrong people in power and keeping the poor people in their place. But now the country seemed to be at war with itself. As opportunities went, this could be a big one for an ambitious gangster. Escobar might not yet appreciate the political ramifications of the unrest but at the very least he might realise that it meant more space in which to operate.

What, Pat wondered, were the limits to Escobar's ambitions? Surely, he had already seen that money brought power? But what if Escobar realised what you could achieve if you combined money with political power? He might become unstoppable.

CHAPTER 15: LIKE FATHERS LIKE SON

For every child, the first day of school is a memorable occasion. The new uniform, some tears perhaps, a certain apprehension. I was no different. But my first day at school sticks in my memory for another reason. I was the only child who arrived in an armoured car.

Soon after the drama of the kidnap attempt, we left the country for what was becoming an annual holiday to Florida and then the UK. Monique had recovered from her recent illness and joined us. While we were away, the army had put down the civil unrest, the armed paramilitary M-19 group retreated to the countryside, Pastrana got on with the job of running the country and, on our return, my parents enrolled me at an Anglo-Colombian bilingual private school in Bogotá. The institution was attended by children of the privileged few, including many of the ruling elite of Colombia. Among recent pupils was Virginia Vallejo, who would go on to become one of the more prominent members of Bogotá high society. Among her many attributes was, according to her yearbook, a 'creative imagination', but it was her flare for journalism that led her eventually to interview and then to become involved with my biological father, a relationship that would become the subject of a book and a Hollywood movie.

It wasn't only the armoured car that marked me out as different to my peers in my class: the other children also seemed a good bit bigger. No explanation was forthcoming and under any other circumstances I might have developed an inferiority complex but, with my godfather Gregorio being the chairman of the school board, the opposite was true. I felt extra-special. And that was before I realised the influence I was able to wield. Now that the controversy of his presidential election was in the past, Pastrana resumed his visits to our house to meet my father. During one of these get-togethers he summoned me to him and gave me his usual greeting.

'*Mi amigo*, don Felipe. Tell me, how are you enjoying school?'

'It's OK,' I said, 'but I wish we could have Coca-Cola for our lunchtime drink instead of milk or water.'

'Well?' The president turned to don Gregorio. 'Can this be arranged?'

Gregorio nodded and smiled.

Later that week at school, my classmates were amazed to see bottles of Coke arrive for lunch. For a brief moment my popularity soared, until the headmaster, who was also a friend of my parents, had a word with them about it when he paid a visit to the house. The Coke option might have been short-lived but the feeling I had of getting my own way certainly wasn't. My year teacher had no chance to rule over me with my godfather as chairman. I completely played up to my exulted status and, as far I was concerned, homework was something other children had to do. I was more engrossed in the latest craze, which at the time was collecting and playing marbles. The whole school appeared to be gripped by this madness.

My adopted mother seemed to disapprove of just about anything that was fun for kids and I knew I would never be able to gain her support in my marbles enterprise. She carried out stringent checks on me every morning to make sure I was wearing the required uniform and wasn't taking anything I shouldn't into school. To get around this, I used to hide my marbles in my socks and pass the bag with my PE kit to my chauffeur to put in the car, by-passing her checks. Getting the marbles to school was one thing but, as I wasn't particularly the best shot, I had to find another way to increase my collection. What I needed was currency to barter for marbles and the answer came with the eleven o'clock morning break, a time when we all started getting peckish. If I could smuggle in some contraband to exchange for marbles, I thought, I'd soon have a top-notch collection. Back home, biscuits were stored in a tin above the fridge. I figured Otilia, who more supportive of my endeavours, had strategically put them there so I could just about reach them if I stood on a chair. I stole as many as I could and hid them in my PE kit. Sure enough, after trading my black-market biscuits for marbles, I soon had a collection that was the envy of my class. Thankfully, the tin was magically replenished each day so there was always a fresh supply – and it meant my tracks were always covered.

My guards did the school run in the armoured car and, at the end of the day, dropped me off at the servant's entrance so they could have a sneaky cigarette and a coffee in the staff quarters. This gave me the perfect cover under which to smuggle my hoard from another day's hard trading into the house, as I was able to place the bag under Otilia's bed in her room next to the kitchen. I made a point of entering the main house without my shoes so my mother would assume I had come in through the back way to drop my dirty shoes in the kitchen for cleaning.

One afternoon, I was in the process of stashing my ill-gotten gains under the maid's bed when, to my amazement, Dad entered the kitchen. He was never usually home at this time and, on the odd occasion that he was back early, he would head straight upstairs for a siesta after a heavy business lunch. I had been rumbled. I knew I would be for it if Mother found out.

'Sssh,' he said, putting his finger to his lips.

Mother was on the phone and he was using the opportunity to carry out his own raid on the stash of chocolate – a restricted substance because he was trying to maintain his waistline. Our mutual acts of criminality meant that, in this area at least, we were as thick as thieves.

'It must be in your blood,' he said, smiling, patting me on the head. I didn't know it at the time but he was referring to my biological father's genes inside me. I knew my secret was safe.

*

As the tumultuous year drew to close, I thought nothing of the announcement that we were heading to Medellín once more for the new year party. I'd barely remembered the event from twelve months earlier. But as soon as we stepped back into the hotel and made our way into the huge ballroom, with the tables set out in the same formation as they had been the previous time, my senses started tingling. I recalled the strange goings-on with the rough-looking men and my encounter with that one man in particular.

I noticed that this time our table was situated a little further back and Barandiga and Martinez did not leave my side in the early part of the evening, before the music and dancing started. Dad and his friends spent a lot of time in deep discussions with the men from Medellín. Initially, I did not see the man I'd spoken to the previous year. Maybe, I thought, he was not there and I would not have to go through a repeat of that odd meeting. Then, however, I spotted a face I recognised. The tall, slim man from last year was among the group talking to Dad.

The door to the room opened and I somehow sensed, even before anyone entered, that it would be him. He strode in with another man. He looked similar to last time; hair unkempt, casual shirt unbuttoned and loose-fitting trousers. He and his colleague looked like they were engrossed in a conversation but then the man clocked my dad standing ahead of him. He immediately turned to scan the room. His eyes locked with mine and he smiled. I blushed and turned away; I wasn't sure why exactly. When I next looked up he and his companion had joined Dad's group and they were all talking intently.

That night was not much fun for me. I had to stay close to the table, never out of Barandiga's reach. My dad spent a long time talking to the other men. From time to time the man I'd met the year before looked over to me and every time our eyes met, he smiled, something he didn't seem to do with anyone else. At times, the discussions appeared to get quite heated. A few of the men became quite animated. Yet, each time the man saw me his face lightened. I noticed too that when that happened people started to look at me. It made me a little uncomfortable.

After a while Dad returned to the table with the tall slim man I had recognised earlier.

'Son, this is don Silvio. Do you remember? You met him here last year?'

The other man smiled, standing very formally.

'How good it is to see you again. You are getting so tall.' The man bowed stiffly. 'I am here to tell you that don Pablo sends his regrets that he is unable to meet you this time. You remember him, don't you?' I looked across to the group at the front of the room. Don Pablo gave me a little salute. 'Ah, that's good,' Silvio said, following my gaze. 'All things being well we will see you again very soon.'

'OK,' my dad said, which I took to mean Silvio's time was up.

Sure enough, Silvio bade his farewell and strode back to join the others.

Dad smiled and placed a hand on my shoulder. I looked towards don Pablo, but Silvio was stood in the way. By the time he moved, so I could see down that end of the room once more, don Pablo had gone.

*

By the end of my first term the latest craze was yo-yos. Having got one for Christmas that year I was desperate to take it into class to practise my skills. Mum had got wise to my PE bag trick so I had to adapt my strategy. I decided to hide the yo-yo deep in my inside blazer pocket. On the first morning back after the festive break I happily marched out of the door towards my guards and the usual armoured transport to school.

'Wait!' I froze as the menacing sound of Mother's voice echoed across the drive. I turned and saw her finger pointing at me. This was it. I had lost my newly acquired Christmas present for good. 'You've forgotten something.' It was my blazer. I'd left the house without even putting it on. Immensely relieved, I retrieved it and got into the armoured car. I couldn't have planned it better.

It was a half-hour drive to school from the house but, although I enjoyed my trips in the fortified vehicle, it was claustrophobic. The windows were only very small and bulletproof and did not open. The green tint of the glass made for a slightly strange atmosphere but I always relaxed once we had driven down the road and were out of sight of the house, as the radio would go on and my escorts would toss their caps to the little back bench behind the seats. The radio blared out the sound of merengue and the mood would lighten.

One morning, however, the formal caps stayed on and the radio remained silent. I was about to question what was going on when I noticed we had taken a detour. We were heading into one of the slum barrios on the outskirts of Bogotá and I started to feel uneasy. Even at my young age I knew this was considered bandit country; the poverty was evident once we swapped the wide boulevards for the narrow unpaved streets. What was going on?

Martinez seemed to know what he was doing as we whizzed through the alleyways before stopping outside a small house in a little row of shacks on the street. There was something familiar about the house but I remained silent as I waited to see what was going to happen next. People were starting to stare and gather round. The sight of an armoured car in this part of town wouldn't have been something the locals were used to. Barandiga picked up a hand-held microphone attached to the radio transmitter via a black, coiled cable, like the one on our telephone at home. As he spoke, he leaned back and tapped out a signal on the door that connected the rear compartment of the truck with the driver and front-seated guard. The solid steel door, to my amazement, revolved to reveal a third guard I hadn't even known was there, sitting on a steel bench to one side of this rear compartment. I could see two men running towards us from the little house, carrying a large, shiny, steel box. It must have been full, as the two men visibly struggled with its weight. There was a loud knock on the side of the truck and the guard got up and opened a compartment that allowed cargo to be loaded without the guards having to run the risk of opening a door. As soon as the box was on board, the cubicle closed and we sped off, leaving the delivery boys engulfed in a hail of dust. In a matter of moments, we had rejoined the main road and it wasn't long before we reached the school. Barandiga escorted me personally to the teacher, and only when I was in the hands of the other adult was I allowed to go and sit with the rest of my classmates for registration.

It wouldn't be the only time my school runs factored in a little detour to collect a delivery. It would be years before I discovered why these extra collections had to be done on a run that was unregistered with De La Rue's manifest. With the company's legitimate cash runs all accounted for and recorded, and drivers required to radio their location into head office to ensure they stuck to their agreed timetable, it was imperative that Dad's special collections were not included in the official business side of the armoured car business.

Knowledge of these collections, their precise locations and destinations, were restricted to a trusted few. The political unrest had only interrupted work for a short while: Operation Durazno was well and truly up-and-running.

CHAPTER 16: SPIRITED AWAY

Anglo-Colombian School, Bogotá, 1971

It was something that required nerves of steel. One slip-up and I would be in trouble. At the very least it could mean a slap on the face; at worst, a visit to the headmaster's office. I weighed up the risk – and figured the reward was worth it.

'You're crazy,' my best mate Hernando said. 'You'll never manage it.'

That was all the further motivation I needed. I flicked the yo-yo to its full length, flipped my wrist up at just the right moment and dragged the toy back. As planned, it snagged on the skirt of the girl in front, yanking it upwards, before the yo-yo snapped back into my palm.

'Who was that?!' The girl turned amid a wailing of laughter from the rest of my mates.

My red face would have given me away, if I'd hung around long enough to be identified as the guilty party. Long before that could happen I ducked out of the way into the crowd of boys, Hernando close behind. 'Well?' I said, when we thought we were out of harm's way. 'Did you see anything?'

'I've no idea,' he said. 'It all happened too fast.'

Neither of us had any clue what the girls kept under their skirts but the temptation to find out was almost as overpowering as the urge to play with our new toys when we should be paying attention to our schoolwork.

My teacher, Miss Susan, had a stern instruction for me once we'd filed back into class after our mid-morning break. 'The headmaster would like to see you.'

I gulped. I'd done it this time. Someone must have given me up. As I trudged down the corridor to his office, the yo-yo burning a hole in my pocket, I contemplated what punishment might await me. What was the sentence for having a toy in school and, worse, using it to torment girls? A letter home to my mother? Expulsion? Both seemed as bad as each other.

'Phillip, take a seat,' the headmaster said when I arrived, shaking. His solemn expression gave nothing away, save for the obvious seriousness of the situation. 'I have to say I am quite sad.' Oh, no, I thought, he's going for the guilt trip. I braced myself for the, 'How you've fallen short of the standards expected of me' lecture. 'It is a shame to be losing you so soon,' he went on. I gulped, a bead of sweat trickled down my spine. Surely he wasn't serious? For one little transgression? 'However, I dare say you will enjoy your time at your new school. You have made quite an impression in your short time with us and I can safely say our loss will be St Hugh's gain.'

I didn't take in much of what was said after that. On one level I was relieved not to be in trouble, but a new school? Whatever could he mean? I was having so much fun and had made lots of friends. Surely there was some mistake. I didn't say anything to my bodyguards and my parents didn't let on anything was different when I got home so I put it down to the head teacher being mistaken.

This was no mix-up, however. Little did I know that my father and Gregorio had hatched a secret plan to get me out of Colombia to a boarding school in England, somewhere they believed I would be safe from further kidnap attempts. Their set-up with my natural father might be already bearing fruit but it was an uneasy truce – one that threatened to flare up at any moment. Better to get me out of harm's way while they still could. Joan was almost as much in the dark as I was. While she knew, of course, of their plans to spirit me away, she remained ignorant of the most recent raid on the house and the likelihood of a repeat.

Not that I was told any of this at the time, of course. Knowing nothing, I kept quiet, hoping that talk of a new school was all a misunderstanding and I could get on with my life. When the term ended my parents told my sister and I that we were going to Florida for Easter and then onto London. We were excited – this meant fun times with Uncle George and Aunt Betty in Boca Raton and, most likely, a trip to the legendary Hamleys toy store when we reached England.

I must have been harbouring a sense of impending doom, however, as by the time we landed in gloomy Heathrow, the weather matched my mood. I was already pining for Florida and the trips to see 'Uncle Walt', as Betty called our regular trips to the Disney theme park. I even missed the annoying Vietnam War news updates interrupting our evening's viewing of *The Flintstones*. Those fading memories were what kept me going as we sat in the smelly old black cab on our way to May's – as I viewed her, the old lady with the haunted house. I thought the only thing I had to look forward to, besides a trip into the centre of London at some point, was the food we never got in Colombia. May made delicious bangers, mash and peas and, on Fridays, the tradition was to spread out breadcrumbs in which to dip enormous pieces of egg-coated fish for frying.

One of our parents would usually take either Monique or me into town to do some shopping. When my mother announced one morning that it was me she was taking to the West End I thought it could only mean one thing – Hamleys. I was gutted, therefore, when our cab pulled up outside an imposing shop on nearby Oxford Street, without a toy in sight. Mum dragged me through a flagship outpost of the John Lewis department store, fighting her way through throngs of people. We had to steer our way through obstacles I'd never seen before, such as escalators. I swiftly discovered that jumping on the moving stairway was the easy bit and getting off was another thing altogether. Eventually, we reached an enormous room packed with kids of all ages trying on school uniforms.

Mother led me to a counter, where a cheerful old gentlemen with a tape measure dangling from his neck asked me if I was excited to be going to my new school.

So it *was* true.

Mother shrugged at having kept it quiet. 'We'd have never got you in the cab if we'd told you.'

The school uniform department of John Lewis in Oxford Street specialised in catering for the international pupil, and the changing rooms were full of children from all corners of the world. I wondered if they had all been kept in the dark as much as me. As soon as the assistant showed me the pink and grey uniform I would be wearing, I began mourning for the dark green of the Anglo-Colombian School.

'He's small for his age,' the man said as he took my measurements. Again, Mother shrugged. What else were they not telling me?

I did get that trip to nearby Hamleys afterwards, which distracted me from thinking too much about a new school, but Hamleys with Mother meant there was still some tension in the air. While I wanted to look at everything, she would rather I chose the first thing I saw so we could get out of there. What a marked difference it was to when Gregorio would occasionally take me shopping in Bogotá. On those occasions money was no object. I was free to choose something, no matter the price or the size. Whenever I was with Mum or Dad, however, I knew to rein it in. After a lengthy trawl through the various floors I settled on a box of Lego and Mum hastily marched me out of the store before I changed my mind.

I expected us to hail a cab back to Swiss Cottage but, instead, Mum led me down Regent Street to a building with a shiny revolving door. She introduced me to a genial older man standing outside and wearing a bright red coat and large black top hat. As he leant down to say, 'Hello,' he reached into his pocket and his white-gloved hand produced an assortment of sweets. I chose one and thanked him. The commissionaire must have known who we were as he swung open the door while he chatted away to Mother. In the sumptuous, marble-clad lobby a smartly dressed lady greeted us. She was about Mother's age and was very well spoken.

'Well, young Phillip, how splendid to see you here,' she said.

Her shiny pearl necklace distracted my gaze but I dutifully shook her hand. I'd met enough grown-ups in formal settings to know how to conduct myself. As she took my hand, Mother told me this was Lady Anne, who worked with my dad.

'I see you've been shopping,' she said, as we entered the lift. 'You can open that upstairs if you like.'

When we reached our floor and the doors opened, I had the most unexpected surprise. Dad and Gregorio were waiting to greet me. I couldn't contain my excitement, diving towards them for hugs. My mood quickly darkened though, as Dad said: 'What did you think of your new uniform?'

'I don't like pink,' I said, to the amusement of the grown-ups. I couldn't see what was funny though. 'Why do I have to go to a new school?'

'We'll talk about it later,' Dad said and I knew the conversation was closed.

After a few minutes, another man emerged through a large, panelled door. He seemed as old as the doorman outside, but more distinguished and a sparkle in his eyes. This was Sir Arthur: everyone called him Gerry. He acknowledged me but seemed to view a child playing with Lego with some bemusement. The adults retreated to Sir Arthur's office behind the panelled door, leaving me with Lady Anne. She brought me a glass of milk while I played on the large, green leather chair by her desk. She tapped away on her typewriter and answered the phone. I must have sat there for hours before Mother emerged from Sir Arthur's office alone. There must have been some outstanding business for the men to discuss in private but she took the opportunity to sit with me and explain a little more about my new school.

To my horror, she said I wouldn't be going home with the family when our holiday ended. I was to remain here in England. My destination was a boarding school and I would be staying there for the entire term. When the school broke up for summer I would go home and see my family again. It was almost too much to take in. I would be leaving my friends and everything I knew in Colombia. No more school runs in the armoured cars, no more mucking around with Hernando. I was devastated.

'Your father and I think it is for your own good,' She went on, giving little away to her own feelings. Part of me suspected she quite liked this arrangement, as I often got the feeling I was perhaps more hassle than she'd anticipated. But my dad? Did he really want to send me away? Was it something I had done?

My head was spinning with the implications of this bombshell when the door opened and the men streamed out. Soon we were all heading down towards the lobby. As we made to leave, Gregorio got down to my level. 'Farewell *mi amigo*,' he said, shaking his head slightly. "This is only a temporary home. Your heart will remain in Colombia.'

I didn't want to say goodbye to don Gregorio. He was my friend. I felt a great sense of attachment to this man who I had grown to trust as my protector. I could however, sense friction, when it came to my welfare, between my adopted mother and Gregorio. They obviously disagreed on the best way to bring me up. He might have signed up to this but I felt on some level he wanted me close to him in Colombia and not thousands of miles away in England.

We had a quiet cab ride back to May's. Once we got there my parents sat me down and tried to sell the idea to me. It was for my future prospects, they said. The schools in England were infinitely better to the one in Colombia and my education was important. Their words didn't make it any easier though. I hadn't realised what all this entailed and it hadn't dawned on me that I would be away from home for weeks on end. Just the thought of being taken away from all that I knew in Bogotá made me feel that my little world was about to collapse around me. At my age, I would not understand the real reasons for all this commotion, and I was just expected to accept it as if it was a normal part of growing up. I couldn't understand why I had to stay here when my little sister was going home. It was to get worse, however.

Why, I asked, were people frequently making comments about how small I was? And why were people in my class so much bigger than me?

My parents exchanged looks. Dad cleared his throat and there was a lengthy pause before he spoke. 'The reason for that,' he said, 'is because there was a complication over your exact date of birth.' What? What was he talking about? Surely they knew the day I was born? 'When you came to us there was no precise record of your birth.'

I didn't understand what he was saying. The look on my face must have said it all, for Mother placed a hand on my knee and said to Dad, 'You better tell him.' Tell me what?! This was rapidly turning into the worst day ever.

'We adopted you,' my dad said, softly. 'Your mum and I are not your real parents.'

He paused for a moment to let those words sink in, but I could only stare blankly, unable to comprehend what I was hearing.

'You were in an orphanage when we found you. Your mother had sadly died, not long after you were born and nothing was known about your father. We wanted to give you a home so you came to live with us.'

I wanted to cry but no tears would come. I just sat there, trying to process this information. Astonishingly, on some level, it wasn't surprising. I had somehow always known I was a bit different. I had always felt my mother was detached in some way from me. Then there was the arrival of my sister, which didn't strike me as normal.

'It doesn't mean we loved you any less. We've always looked on you as our own son. We love you as much as if you were our own,' Dad said. Mum nodded, seemingly content to let him do all the talking.

'What happened to my real Mum and Dad?'

Mum looked at Dad but he didn't return her glance. He shrugged. 'No one really knows for sure what happened to them. All that's known is that your mum died and so you became an orphan.'

Then the tears came. I'm not sure if I was weeping for the mother I would never know or whether the emotion prompted by hearing this was just too much for me. Once I started welling up it felt impossible to make my tears stop. My poor mother, what had happened to her? And my adoptive family . . . did this mean they had stopped loving me because they were sending me away now? It was all very confusing.

They cuddled me for a while and slowly I calmed down and eventually ran out of tears to cry. 'So, what does that mean about my birth?'

Dad explained that, when they were applying for my passport, they had made a mistake. At the time, a temporary British passport could only be issued to a child providing they had been adopted for a minimum of five years. According to my official baptism document, I was born in August 1965. Back then it was common to register the birth of an orphan with the local Catholic church charged with the care of the minor. I had been rescued and taken almost immediately to my home via the orphanage. In 1967 I had only been living with them for two years. The paperwork for my adoption had only just started to be processed before we left for England. The simplest solution, Dad said, to allow them to be able to get me a passport straight away, was to adjust my date of birth by three years. If they hadn't done this our trip to England to obtain my British citizenship would have been delayed considerably and the plans to pack me off to boarding school as early as possible would have been put on hold. No documentation was required; they just had to sign a declaration. At least I now knew why I had been so much smaller than my friends at school in Colombia, even if I didn't completely understand the logic. This little alteration, however innocent or otherwise at the time, was to have an lasting effect on my life as I was growing up, and particularly at school, where I was always playing catch-up with my much bigger and older class mates.

If I had been bewildered before, it was nothing to how I felt now.

Fearing I might sink into a pit of despair, they suggested taking us to the cinema, where the musical *Oliver!* was showing. In hindsight it probably wasn't the best choice of movie. I found myself identifying with the plight of Oliver Twist. Had I been a boy for sale? Was it true that my adoptive parents could love me as much as my real mother might have?

The next three weeks at Swiss Cottage flew by, despite me wanting them to drag out as long as possible. Eventually the day came and it was time to make the trip I had been dreading, to St Hugh's preparatory school near Faringdon, Oxfordshire. The school had moved to Carswell Manor just after the Second World War. It was such an old building that it was listed in William the Conqueror's *Domesday Book*. Everything about the place made me feel I was entering the old house in *The Addams Family* series I had watched on Aunt Betty's kitchen telly. In a damp, cobwebbed porch, a very serious-looking, thin man welcomed us. He was the headmaster, Mr Young, and he led us up a creaky, black-stained oak staircase. The house and this man gave me the creeps and, when I caught the sound of hundreds of children from the large room that led off the hallway, I pictured the workhouse of *Oliver!* Was this going to be my life? Begging for scraps to eat? This was a living nightmare.

Mum and Dad had a chat with the headmaster and his deputy, Mr Barnes, but it was all too brief. Soon it was time for them to leave. My whole being seemed to ache with a deep sense of abandonment, standing on the gravel drive. I tried desperately to hold back the tears but the floodgates opened. I felt a pain in my chest so acute it was like my heart had stopped. I was confused about my own identity but was still distraught at watching the only people I could call family fade away into the distance. I already missed them terribly but cursed them for the knowledge they'd dumped on me and for leaving me in this dreadful old place in a foreign country, thousands of miles from home, away from everyone I loved.

A kindly matron gave me a few moments to compose myself and then led me upstairs to the dormitory that was to be my home from now on. For the rest of that afternoon I was inconsolable, as anger, confusion and frustration raged through me. No matter what the matron tried, I refused to do or go anywhere. My mind was in turmoil. Only now was it sinking in what my parents had told me; that I was adopted. Were they still my parents? Did I need to call them anything different? I felt so mixed up. I always thought Dad was my father and yet now I knew there might be someone out there who had a proper claim to that title. Would I ever meet him? If so, what would that mean? What if I didn't like this person? I wanted everything to go back to the way it had been before, when I didn't know.

That evening the other kids in my dorm arrived for bath time, which helped a bit and I started emerging from my shell. I resolved, however, not to tell them the truth about my parentage. I didn't want them to think I was different. I just tried to put it to the back of my mind and it wasn't long before the antics of my new classmates made me feel a bit better. When I went to bed that night, however, my dreams were plagued by dark images. I had the sense of the young woman in red. She was in pain and crying and there was nothing I could do. There were loud bangs and smoke, and I woke panting, scared and confused. I lay awake most of that night, my imagination running wild, listening to the sounds of other boys moaning or crying in their sleep and the strange noises from the other dorms. By morning, though, I resolved that if I was going to survive in this house of horrors I was going to have to live by my wits.

And so, over the next few weeks, my new life at boarding school became a series of discoveries. Lessons here were of a totally different nature to anything I'd experienced at home in Colombia. At St Hugh's we had to behave and do as we were told or we would be sent up to Mr Young. In his study he had a worn leather chair near the large window overlooking the playing fields. This, I soon discovered, was the beating chair, over which naughty boys had to bend to have the living daylights thrashed out of them with a hard-wooden hairbrush. As soon as I heard about this, I focused my mind on finding out how far I could push things without ending up in there. Learning how to get what I wanted without getting caught was my new hobby. I quickly developed unparalleled skills in the art of deception and cunning. If I needed to plant evidence of any wrongdoing in other boys' pockets to divert suspicion away from me then so be it – the threat of Mr Young's brutal corporal punishment didn't make my peers and I better behaved, just better at not getting caught.

Despite my newfound skills, the frustration of not getting my way and having strange adults telling me what to do all the time took its toll on my usually pleasant demeanour.

I found learning English particularly difficult. It would be safe to say that first term at boarding school was not among the happiest times of my life. There were a few silver linings to this dismally grey cloud, however. In Colombia, football was the number one sport. But at St Hugh's rugby was the name of the game. I took to it, mainly because it entailed smashing the complete living daylights out of everyone (all perfectly legitimately and within the rules, of course). Boys being boys we treated these rules with a certain lack of respect. As far as I was concerned all rules were there to be broken – provided you didn't get spotted. Our ref, Mr Snow, was the French teacher and games-master. Clearly, he loved the sport and greatly encouraged us all. He was also someone you didn't want to cross and he was able to keep us in line while earning our respect. Those early weeks learning the art of the great game of rugby would prove to be my saving activity, all those miles away from home. I was able to channel my pent-up frustration. And, afterwards, following a hot shower and dinner, I found I was able to cope with the otherwise miserable life I found myself in.

The other novel experience of my first term was the sight and the horrendously loud noise of a strange-looking aircraft that flew low overhead from the nearby RAF base Brize Norton at the same time, 3 p.m. every weekday. It was making test flights for the first supersonic passenger jet, Concorde. The pilots swooped so low that they sometimes sent one or two lead-lined windows smashing to the ground.

As I reluctantly settled into life at boarding school, I discovered routine was the key to understanding how the place ran. During the week we shuffled about the school like zombies in a little prison. Mercifully, Sunday afternoons were our free time. As soon as we got the signal we fled as fast as possible to the woods and as far away from the eyes of the headmaster as we could get. We were isolated from the outside world and I started to feel as if the privately educated, English boarder was some sort of tribal species.

We forged allegiances and recreated pitched battles we'd seen in cowboy films. Deep in the woods we built camps from sticks and piles of wet leaves and we mounted ferocious defences. With hastily fashioned bows and genuinely sharp arrows, heavily armed patrols were sent out to intercept intruders. Any group of badly camouflaged, enemy fighters would be given the option to immediately surrender. If they refused, a battle would commence until all the ammunition was exhausted. There never seemed to be any victors. I wondered what the matron made of the sudden influx of casualties to the sick bay, all arriving with tales of accidental falls in the woods while 'treasure-hunting' or the like. It was a miracle no one was seriously hurt or killed during those Sunday afternoon battles. They helped take our minds off the isolation.

A crash course in decimal currency, which had just come into being in the UK earlier that year, brought that difficult first term to an end. Finally, I was going to be reunited with my family and the promise of another glorious summer holiday in Florida and the chance to return home to Colombia had kept me going. A cousin of mine on my mother's side called Peter was coming to collect me. We spent a night in his house in Surrey before he delivered me to Heathrow airport the following day. BOAC operated an 'auntie' service, where staff helped to get unaccompanied, overseas school children to their parents for the holidays. We were all shepherded into a pen in terminal three while an airhostess meticulously checked all the labels and identities of some thirty, over-excited children destined for all four corners of the globe on different flights. Given how used I was to flying by then it was hard to appreciate that this was a time when children rarely flew anywhere. Transatlantic flights remained the reserve of the privileged few with our designated auntie whizzing us through all the various checking points without having to queue; we were always the first to get on the plane. My flight took in Antigua and

Caracas before reaching Colombia and heading on to the eastern side of South America. I was put to the back of the plane with the other unaccompanied children but, while others fidgeted and made a nuisance of themselves with other passengers, I sat contemplating what might await me in Bogotá. In her letters to me, my mother – I still thought of them as my parents, despite their revelations – had made mention of a new house they were going to buy. It seemed that everything was changing.

When we touched down in Antigua, around half the passengers disembarked and our auntie allowed me to step onto the boarding stairs to take in some real Caribbean air. I caught a blast of heat that reminded me of Florida. After a short hop to the Venezuelan capital, we finally headed to Bogotá. As we descended over the large mountain range that almost completely encircled the plateau on which the city stood, through the dense tropical cloud cover, I recalled my dad telling me that only the most experienced pilots were permitted to land here. The perilous landscape had caused a few planes to come a cropper over the years. Dad said poverty was so prevalent in the shanty villages on the flight path that any valuables were stripped from the crash sites long before the emergency crews could get there. I thought of how lucky we were to live in relative luxury but then wondered about my own meagre possessions on this flight. A pink, public school uniform would be considered lean pickings should this plane go down.

Fortunately, we landed safely and, as we taxied towards our stand, the pilot apologised for asking the passengers to wait in their seats for a minute in order to allow a VIP passenger to disembark safely. This was my cue. My auntie escorted me forward to the steps and I was greeted by the familiar sound of the siren as our black Chevrolet came into view. As usual, an open-top army jeep, full of soldiers with white MP armbands, followed. The moment the small cavalcade pulled up at the bottom of the steps, Dad jumped out, accompanied by Barandiga. I couldn't wait any more. Escaping the grip of my stewardess, I ran as fast as I could down the steps.

'Hey, welcome home,' said Dad. 'I've missed you.'

After a big hug and a kiss, I jumped in the back. I knew I'd have the seats to myself with all my stuff as Mother didn't much care for all that driving around with sirens or soldiers. She felt much more at home at the women's guild afternoon tea party or coffee mornings at the British embassy. Instantly, I felt I was back where I belonged.

Arriving at De La Rue's headquarters in Avenida de Las Américas, the guards stood to attention and the massive metal gate opened. Gregorio, the customary cigar hanging from his mouth, was waiting to greet me in the reception area. This was a lovely surprise and I stayed for a few hours in Dad's office talking to his secretary, whose name, Sexta, made me blush. She was unlike any woman I'd ever seen before, much younger than Lady Anne, and stunning in a very short, bright, pinafore dress and massive, multi-coloured striped platform heels and sporting a bouffant hairstyle. She spoke perfect English, Spanish and French and could simultaneously talk on the phone, smoke a cigarette, drink a cup of coffee and listen to the radio while typing a letter at lightning speed.

Having concluded his business meeting with the don, Dad collected me and we made our way home. I was looking forward to renewing the now distant relationship with my little sister and to seeing Otilia and my mother again, but having the privacy of my own bedroom again was what I longed for the most. As we drove home, the reassuring smell of tobacco wafting through from the front of the car, mingling with the scent of the leather upholstery, brought home how fantastic it was to be back home.

For the first few days we fell into the old routine, with Saturdays spent on the golf course and lazy Sundays. The atmosphere changed, however, as Dad broke the news that we were expecting the president. It was only a few days before my birthday, in August 1971 (by then even I had lost track of how old I really was, as compared to the age I was supposed to be). On the afternoon of the visit, we returned home from a long day at the golf club with Chalky (Dad's *James Bond* 'Q') and Sir Arthur, who had travelled over from London. As we turned in to our street, I noticed a group of soldiers disembarking from an army truck, several police motorbikes and a couple of imposing black cars outside our home. My parents were noticeably apprehensive. They didn't like these visits. It made them feel uncomfortable when Pastrana's entourage took over the house. I felt for Otilia, as she always seemed to be on the receiving end of some kind of scolding from my mother on these stressful occasions. As soon as we entered the first floor lounge a loud voice greeted me.

'Ah, *mi amigo* don Felipe.' It was hard, when he was making such a fuss of me, to remember he was the most important politician in the land. 'Have you been behaving yourself at your new school?'

I nodded and smiled, as his assistants and security personnel milled around in the background with my parents, while Gregorio and the president talked to me. It was as if my parents had been sidelined. Pastrana never stayed very long during his visits, and that too was the case this time. Before he stood up to leave, he leaned over and whispered in my ear. 'I have a special gift for you that you will see in a few days when you go to a particular place.'

Intrigued by what he could mean, I looked to my dad, who just shrugged. I should have known that all would be revealed in good time.

'Do we have to have our privacy invaded in such dramatic fashion?' my mother said, when the entourage had swept back out of the house.

'He is the president of Colombia,' my dad replied. 'You don't have a choice in the matter.' My mother looked stunned at this response, and it was a shock for me too to see Dad silence her for once.

At times I felt my parents made an odd couple. He was quite maverick at times and also easy-going while she seemed uptight and rigid. She often referred to the Colombian people in an unnecessarily unpleasant manner. The locals were always 'those people'.

The following day Martinez drove us to what I thought was a farm. In fact, it was the military riding school of Surala, on the outskirts of Bogotá. Members of staff dressed in riding britches and white shirts greeted us with great ceremony, having been warned of our imminent arrival. I was still wondering what was going on as my dad led me to a paddock in which stood a magnificent-looking horse.

'Your gift from the president.' I couldn't believe it. A horse. For me? '"Phillip", in ancient Greek, means "friend of the horses" – so it is very fitting,' Dad explained.

The horse was mine to name and, continuing the Greek theme, I called him Achilles because he had one white heel. Standing with him was a very tall, thin man in shiny, black, knee-length boots and white riding britches, carrying a whip. Dad explained this was Colonel Savogar of the Colombian army, who was a good friend of De La Rue and would look after Achilles for me.

Savogar had Achilles saddled up and took me for my first little ride on my very own horse. It was the beginning of twice-weekly trips to the riding school for lessons. As I became more at home in the saddle, I loved the feeling of the wind in my face, as we picked up pace and I was able to keep a steady gallop. If I thought that was thrilling, it was nothing compared to the next ride Dad had in store for me.

CHAPTER 17: MOVING THE MONEY

Bogotá, summer 1971

The first I knew something was happening was when Otilia shook me awake.

'Hurry, get up and get dressed. You're going out with your father.'

I didn't need telling twice. I had come to learn very quickly that this must mean something exciting would happen and I wasn't disappointed at missing my lie-in. I jumped out of bed and got ready as fast as I could.

Dad, as usual, kept his cards close to his chest, only offering just the hint of a smile when I asked what we were doing. I imagined he didn't want to tell me in case I let something slip to Mother and she put a stop to it. We jumped in the Chevrolet with Martinez and Barandiga, while the team of security officers provided their escort.

As we headed out of Bogotá, I sensed something special was in the offing. We rarely drove out of town and I started to feel my excitement build. We drove for a few minutes until we arrived at a small airfield not far from the city's perimeter. We drove into a fenced-off area and at the sight of two helicopters five hundred metres away, their rotor blades slowly turning, I jumped forward.

'Are we going in those?'

Dad just smiled. The first helicopter was a small machine that had room for two passengers squeezed next to the pilot. The second chopper was much bigger, a UH-1 'Huey' green army helicopter with the Colombian flag on the tail. It was soon full and started to take off. I sat, transfixed, mesmerised by the noise. A soldier opened the car door, reached in and picked me up with both hands. Dad and the bodyguards were already hurrying towards the helicopter. By the time the soldier had carried me across the grass, battling the wind, my father was already in position by the pilot. The door slammed shut and, in seconds, we were airborne. The ground rapidly retreated as we rose, effortlessly, towards the clouds. There was a small window in the floor, and I loved looking at the tiny houses below us. The pilot and Dad had communication devices and it was obvious that they were engaged in a conversation. I didn't care, I was just transfixed by the world whizzing by beneath my feet. The bigger army helicopter was ahead of us and one of the soldiers rested his feet on the exterior machine gun mounting. His helmet with the dark visor made him look like a giant insect.

Soon we left the urban sprawl of Bogotá far behind us and were soaring over the mountains. There was little time to admire the view. The chopper lurched down into a deep valley, plunging us into thick, low cloud. The precarious descent was no fun, and I clung to my seat, though the blind-flying only lasted a few seconds before we broke through the cover and, to my relief, we were soon almost clipping the tops of the trees as a seemingly endless carpet of green stretched out into the distance.

The tone of our machine changed to a much deeper sound, and I watched as the ground closed rapidly. A small clearing was now visible and some small figures waved orange flags at us. Suddenly, we were on the ground, in what looked like a large garden with a white, bungalow farmhouse at the end of a path that led to our landing area. As everyone jumped out I was nervous about following, scared that the blades would take off the top of my head. I needed a little encouragement to climb down. Dad was already on the grass, striding to meet several men who appeared from the farmhouse carrying a large, tin box.

I watched as the men noisily crammed the box under the seat I had just vacated.

'What's that?' I shouted at Dad.

'Just something we have to collect.'

That was typical of Dad – answering the question while still keeping me in the dark.

The bungalow, I could now see, was surrounded by landscaped gardens and thick shrubbery. Two men directed us away from the path to the side of the bungalow and a little walled garden. We were obviously expected, as our host, who did not readily identify himself, introduced us to a man and a woman waiting in the garden. As soon as I saw them, I recognised the man. I had met him in Medellín . . . not the one I'd spoken with a year before but his friend, Silvio.

'Ah, it is so good to see you, young Felipe.' The woman I assumed to be his wife was slim, with bouffant dark hair. She had a warm smile. 'Do you remember being here before?' Silvio said.

I looked blankly at Dad. 'Where even are we?' I said.

'Girardot,' Silvio replied. 'You like flying here? I nodded. 'It is a lot better than those mountain roads. Probably safer too,' he said, looking at our armed guards.

'He is too young to remember. It was a long time ago,' Dad said to Silvio. To me, he added: 'I drove you out here once before. You were very little.'

'Not so any more,' Silvio said, stepping back as if to admire me. 'My friend will want to know how big you have grown. Let me take a photo.'

I knew that Silvio was one of Dad's people and I was used to a fuss being made but, as Silvio got his camera there was something strange about it all. He asked me to pose for a picture. I looked at Dad for reassurance and he nodded. I did as I was told but it felt a bit set up.

I could tell when Dad's meetings were for pleasure as well as for business. On the golf course or at the house he was content to while away the hours over a whisky once the work was concluded, but not today. He was now plainly itching to get out of here. Almost as soon as Silvio had taken his picture, Dad motioned for us to head back to the helicopters. This time we departed before our military escort and, in a few moments, we were heading back into the clouds.

As soon as we landed at the airfield, two men wearing the familiar, dark-blue uniform of De La Rue approached and took the box to an armoured truck. Our little convoy headed into Bogotá and I noticed the truck veer off in the direction of Avenida de Las Américas and De La Rue's head office. I could only guess at what was inside that box but it struck me that it was another successful pick-up for what must surely have been the world's most extravagant courier service.

Once we were back at the house I peppered Dad with questions. Why did he take me on that trip? Why did we meet Silvio and why had Silvio wanted to take a photo of me?

Dad sighed and sat down beside me. 'One day I will explain all of this to you,' he said. 'For now, just know that I had to fulfil a request from someone I do business with, which meant meeting Silvio. I knew it was a trip that would be safe enough for you to make and I thought you would enjoy having a trip on a helicopter.' I nodded vigorously. 'As for the picture, Silvio met you some time ago, with some other people, who will be surprised to see how much you've grown.' He paused before adding, 'Sometimes you have to do things in business that you're not entirely comfortable with but it will help in the long run.'

'But who were the people who want to see my picture?'

Dad stood up and raised his hand. The conversation was over. I bit my tongue. I would have to wait for the time, as Dad said, when he would explain to me the significance of all this.

CHAPTER 18: THE RISE OF EL DOCTOR

'He who controls the cash controls the country.' Pat often thought of those words as he watched another delivery safely make its way to De La Rue's HQ.

He knew that once the box of US dollars reached its destination it would be easy to mix the bags in the back of the armoured truck. The cash from the gangs and from the banks became indistinguishable. Which, in effect, they were. Moving the legitimate cash and the illegitimate. That was the business Pat had found himself in. It was all part of the same economy in Colombia. In the time he had been in the country he had asked himself the question, where did you draw the line? It was so blurred. Who was to say what was corrupt and what was not? There were so many bribes and backhanders going around it was impossible for Pat to keep up. Sometimes he felt all they did was move the same money around between the lawful and the criminal operators – and with it the intelligence.

Pat wasn't wholly happy with this arrangement. Transporting the cash was one thing. Influencing the cash generators – the gangsters – was something else. In that regard, 'control' was something he didn't feel he had. Silvio had been JB's contact and he provided the route into an increasingly volatile criminal gang. From what they understood in the intelligence they had received so far, the Medellín mob was making vast amounts of money, more than anyone on the De La Rue side had predicted when they began Operation Durazno. Pat knew that these sums of money would not only make them stronger but more dangerous too.

Until now, Silvio had played the role of the ideal informant, the go-between, and he was being amply rewarded for his efforts, but Pat suspected he was only telling them half the story of Pablo Escobar's operations. As reported through JB, Silvio was keen to play down Pablo's expansion but Pat could see for himself – by the money that De La Rue alone handled – that they were surely cornering the cocaine market. He knew he would feel a lot better if he could get closer to the main man in that operation – Pablo Escobar. Cut out the middleman. Deal face-to-face – *de hombre a hombre* – with the man Pat heard people in Medellín were now calling 'El Doctor'.

According to sources, in the summer of 1971 Escobar was behind the kidnapping of a wealthy textile factory owner, Diego Echavarria. He was a high-profile figure, with a successful business and an expanding property empire, feted in polite society because he appeared every bit the caring philanthropist, funding a number of projects in his native city, Itagüí, and throughout Antioquia. Most notably he had gained plaudits and sympathy for opening a school and an educational foundation in honour of his daughter, Isolda, who had died of a rare condition. The kidnap heaped further torment on his family.

That the Echavarria family had the funds to pay the $50,000 ransom was not in question. They would have paid double that to have him back alive and well. But in the weeks he was held hostage another story began to emerge, that Echavarria's success owed much to the exploitation of his workforce. Factory workers – those who still had a job – complained of terrible conditions and pay. They said the reason he was able to expand his property empire and fund his charitable projects was because he was squeezing the ordinary people out of every peso. Those who had the terrible jobs were the lucky ones, however. Many workers had been laid off as advances in technology made them superfluous. At the same time, factory expansion meant that farmers had been evicted from their land and ordered to move into city slums.

When news of Echavarria's kidnapping reached the slum-dwellers' ears, they rejoiced and this unexpected situation left the gang with a dilemma. The ransom was duly paid, but should they simply return the controversial figure to continue his ransacking of decades' old traditions or take the opportunity to rid the region of a scoundrel?

Pat could well imagine that it wouldn't have taken Escobar and his gang long to decide what to do. This was too good an opportunity to miss. It was a chance to make a statement. When Echavarria was finally found a month later it was in a ditch, his body battered, bearing all the hallmarks of being throttled. For his family, it was devastating. For those workers who felt wronged by him it was justice. For Pablo Escobar, it was a public relations triumph.

When word got out that the body had been dumped not far from where Escobar was born, people assumed he was behind the killing – and they loved him for it. In criminal circles his name was already known but now his reputation was spreading throughout Medellín and Antioquia. For the first time people, recognised a crime had been committed for something more than immediate gain. This was social justice. Who was this man of the people who was willing to stand up for the lowest of the low?

People in the barrios started to call him El Doctor. Pat could well imagine that Escobar had swiftly noticed that the people of Medellín – his people – were crying out for a champion to look out for their interests. Pat wondered if the original plan to kidnap Echavarria was even Escobar's idea. He knew how people's morals could become skewed once they started to attach some kind of moral justification to their criminal acts and, when he heard the details of the murder, part of him didn't want to believe it. Yet, having met the man, deep down he suspected it was all true. And the reaction of the local people? Escobar couldn't have planned it – no one could have foreseen that. Even given Echavarria's poor reputation among his workers, it was off the scale.

The wealthy factory owner's home had been called *el Castillo*, an ostentatious mock Bavarian castle he had built for himself from his ill-gotten gains. Ironically, it wouldn't be long before 'hero-of-the-people' Pablo Escobar created a similar palace for himself, built from his own fortune, amassed from other people's misery.

CHAPTER 19: AN AUDIENCE WITH DON PABLO

Medellín, December 1971

I had been around enough important people to recognise when they changed the atmosphere around them. I could see it in the faces of others – the way they behaved; the way they stood in line, patiently waiting their turn for an audience. I had seen it with Gregorio, I had seen it with Sir Arthur, even with my father . . . and I had definitely seen it with the president of Colombia. And I saw it with *him*.

I knew, as soon as the commotion started and people began acting differently, that someone of great importance was entering. All eyes turned to the doors. In walked three men. Even before I saw the face of the man in the middle I knew who it was. He was not a tall man, by any means, but somehow he now looked bigger. There was an air about him. People seemed to alter their behaviour when he walked towards the tables, gradually stopping what they were doing and moving to be in line to greet him. Just like those other important people in my life, this man commanded respect – and people gave it.

I hadn't been looking forward to the annual new year trip to Medellín at all. The previous time I'd been stuck at a table all night and I couldn't think of anything worse than having to go back for another boring party. My holiday time in Colombia was precious. I missed my life in Bogotá so much that any time taken away from there almost gave me a physical pain. I didn't think there was anything in Medellín for me and I couldn't see why we had to go there. If Dad had business to attend to, which he did there regularly, then why couldn't he just factor in another trip? Why did he have to drag me along?

The night started as usual. I expected to see that little dance the grown-ups performed; the formal greetings, the pleasantries before they shuffled off to a private space for the real discussions. But as the evening progressed I began to get the sense it was going to be different. I didn't have to wait long for that to be confirmed. I could see don Pablo looking over as he usually did. This time, however, when Dad returned to our table it was to collect me.

'I think it would be good for you to meet someone again,' he said as he led me to the front of the room and to what was very much now the head table for the most esteemed guests. Dad kept a reassuring hand on my shoulder and I was aware people were staring at me. As we got closer the men around don Pablo parted to let us through. Now I got a close look at the man I'd only seen from afar twelve months previously. Everything about him looked in sharper focus. His hair was neater and not greasy, his moustache full but trimmed, his clothes casual but better fitted. He didn't crouch down to my level as many adults did, but bowed his head and extended a hand. I caught a whiff of cologne that reminded me of the time I sat at his table, wanting to get back to my dad. Now it seemed strangely intoxicating.

'*Mi amigo*,' he said, sounding exactly like the president, in a deep, gravelly tone. 'I am pleased to see you again.' I shook his hand, conscious that my own palms were sweaty. 'I hear you are at a new school. A long way away. How is it?'

'Good,' I said, looking to Dad, who was still by my side, his hand still resting on my shoulder.

Pablo smiled as though he approved. 'A good education is important. You need to work hard. I would like to go back to school. I didn't work hard enough when I had the chance but I want to change that.' He looked to my dad when he said this.

'That's good to hear,' Dad said. 'You can get an education in lots of ways without going to school or college though.'

'Perhaps, but I want to learn. I want to better myself. I want to become knowledgeable about many things, like you.'

'I have been lucky,' Dad said. 'In England, there are more opportunities to do well.'

Don Pablo nodded. 'Ah yes, England, I want to go there one day. Maybe I will come and visit you at your new school.'

I glanced at Dad just in time to see a serious look flash across his face before he smiled. 'Maybe one day.' Dad went on to say it was time to take me back to our table, where Barandiga and Martinez were waiting with the rest of the family.

'Until next time,' Don Pablo said. 'Even though you are in England, you know where your home is.'

'Yes, Colombia,' I said proudly.

'Medellín,' he said, looking to my father.

He offered a tight smile in return. 'Why did he say that?' I asked as we crossed the hall.

'I think,' Dad said, 'he likes to believe there is nowhere better than Medellín.'

'Is he going to come and visit me?'

We reached the table. Dad sat me down and, with both hands on my shoulders, his eyes locked on mine. 'No. That is not going to happen.'

With that, he turned and made his way back to the front of the room, to where don Pablo was waiting, watching.

CHAPTER 20: THE PRIVATE BANKER

For Pat, the decision to get closer to Pablo Escobar had been, in the end, a no-brainer.

The relationship was improved with the smuggling gang, the delivery runs were fully operational and the intelligence gleaned from their supply routes was exactly what Sir Arthur had been looking for when the germ of the idea was born back in 1959. Pat, never one to rest on his laurels, could see the ambitious young criminal was now the only show in town. Even setting aside their very personal connection, he would have been drawn to him if they were meeting for the first time.

Every year, Escobar had shown himself to be several steps ahead of his peers. How much of that had been down to the interest taken by De La Rue and the company's help in facilitating the gang's plans? Who could say? More importantly, would Pablo Escobar have reached this level of notoriety and wealth in such a short time on his own? Probably. In all his international dealings, Pat had never encountered anyone so single-mindedly ruthless and cunningly complex. It was for those reasons, though, that their meetings unnerved him.

Not one for small talk and often with a detached air that could be explained by the amount of marijuana he smoked, Pablo Escobar was hard to read. When asked outright about the crimes attributed to him, he deflected and, when quizzed about potential next moves, he obfuscated. On one hand his faith in *omertà*, the code of silence, made him the perfect business partner. On the other, if the stories about him were to be believed, his loyalty lasted only as long as you were useful to him. While Pat was giving him, nearly, all that he wanted, relations were smooth. But he did not want to dwell on what might happen should Escobar ever feel he was being crossed.

Pat had to hand it to the Colombian. What had started out as a petty crime outfit had, under his leadership, morphed into a sophisticated smuggling operation and had now become a significant and well-organised business enterprise. It moved huge shipments of a variety of products with increasing ease, largely thanks to JB's connections: his own meteoric rise, through the ranks of the Panamanian security services, had given him a unique position from which to run his double-edged operation. While his legitimate job as an intelligence officer meant he was continually liaising with the CIA, he also had his ambitions, which, Pat suspected, reached as far as the Panamanian presidency. Pat also guess that, as much as JB was passing on useful intel on the smugglers to the Americans, there would be times when information regarding significant shipments was not forthcoming. He imagined for these bouts of forgetfulness JB would have been amply rewarded by Escobar's people.

It was a murky world but at least Pat could console himself that the De La Rue side of the arrangement – converting contraband US dollars into legitimate pesos and funnelling them into the Colombian banking system – had so far run smoothly. It always helped, of course, to have been awarded the one and only contract with the central bank of the republic, which meant that De La Rue could influence the production and distribution levels of currency to the banks. The flow of US currency to the firm's vaults was dictated by demand for redistribution or held and exchanged for newly printed Colombian currency at De La Rue's offices.

This meant that, at any given time, there were enormous quantities of cash being stored in Avenida de Las Américas, where Pat retained a small private army whose role was to guard and facilitate transportation.

And if ever it seemed like there was a danger of too much cash flooding the system, there were experts in London who could fly over to ensure everything was regulated properly. Unless that happened, however, it was down to Pat to ensure everything ran smoothly. He was happy to take care of the contractual arrangements with all the banks, along with the distribution of the local currency around the country. He didn't mind the many long meetings with unsavoury individuals, principally in Medellín and Cali, to organise the integration of the dirty cash coming in on the small aircraft. Gregorio might have smoothed the way and opened the doors to the locals in power but Pat doubted even he knew the true extent of the money being generated. Sir Arthur's instruction from the outset was that the Colombians were not to be let in on Operation Durazno. This command had been followed to the letter. It was the ideal set-up, keeping Gregorio and his people completely in the dark; they were innocent bystanders to any cloak-and-dagger activity.

Pat was not taking any chances. The smugglers' preferred way of working was still to hide large sums of cash at safe houses in the *fincas*. Whether this loot was collected by road or air, its movement still presented security issues. Even with a heavily armed guard you could never be too careful. Often the convoy would take a detour or make an unscheduled stop at a small roadside café or sugar cane plantation to shake off any tails. Safe delivery of the cash showed the smugglers that De La Rue could be trusted and Pat wouldn't have put it past them to set up an ambush just to test the defences. But, so far, so good.

And now, to ensure the young Escobar was onside, Pat wanted to offer him a more specialised service. He told the Colombian that Pablo, as the brains of the operation, needed to be appropriately remunerated. For Pat, it might mean he had to perform a little creative accountancy where the proceeds were concerned but, after all, cash delivery and distribution were his forte. Pat's suggestion was nothing less than he would look after Pablo's money for him. He could skim it off the top of the gang's profits. No one need know. It was to be a private arrangement between them both. This would mean that Escobar would always have access to a secret stash of funds. Escobar didn't need much convincing. He told Pat to set it up right away.

CHAPTER 21: EMPIRE BUILDING

What Pat suspected, but didn't know the full details of, was that Escobar had begun working with a far more successful cocaine dealer, Alvaro Prieto.

A run-in with the law had landed Escobar in jail for a short period. As luck would have it, his cellmate had been Prieto. The pair had hit it off and the drug trafficker had taken his willing student under his wing. For someone desperate to further his education, Escobar couldn't have found a better tutor. Up to that point he had shifted small shipments but nothing from which to build an empire. Prieto had shown him a glimpse of the future. Cocaine was not a drug restricted to the slums and the destitute. It was the narcotic of choice for the fast-living professionals of America's most affluent communities. In Miami, it was finding a market with doctors, lawyers and bankers; anyone craving a taste of the counterculture. It was a party drug like no other.

Once Escobar saw how cocaine was produced, packaged, shipped and sold he decided he didn't just want a slice of the action, but he wanted to run the entire game. For his part, Prieto was only a dealer rather than a producer and Escobar, possibly growing impatient at the slow pace of progress made by his fellow smugglers, decided to take matters into his own hands. According to folklore, he stole a car, drove the 1,300 kilometres to a contact in Ecuador and bought 5 kilograms of imported Peruvian cocaine paste.

Three days later he was back in Medellín and had set up his own means of production to have the paste turned into 14 kilograms of street-ready cocaine.

The biggest exporter in Medellín at the time was Fabio Restrepo. Escobar had no connection with him but he knew criminal contacts who did – the Ochoa brothers. They agreed to arrange a meeting between Escobar and Restrepo. To Restrepo the seasoned trafficker, who shipped about 120 kilograms a year, Escobar must have looked like every other young punk trying to force his way into the burgeoning drug scene. His 14 kilograms by no means made him a big player. Restrepo knew he had a choice – either do business with the smuggler or send him packing, but despite Escobar's smaller stature, he chose the former, agreeing to sell on Escobar's supply. The sale netted Escobar more than a hundred thousand dollars (equivalent to over $500,000 today), more than any other single deal he'd done in his life.

Several things must have struck Pablo Escobar after landing his first proper cocaine deal: he needed someone he could trust to help him move and hide his money; there was potential to form an alliance with the Ochoa brothers to pool their resources; cocaine was the only business worth worrying about and, if was to truly maximise his potential, he needed to eliminate the competition.

CHAPTER 22: CREATING A MONSTER

Pat's trip to the usual *finca* to discuss business with Silvio shouldn't have presented any problems. He elected to have Martinez drive rather than fly and they took an escort on the long run up the winding mountain roads. When he arrived, however, he was surprised to find Silvio was not alone. With him was a stern-faced Pablo Escobar.

'Where's the boy?' The opening gambit took Pat by surprise. There was no greeting, no handshake.

'He's returned to England.' A scowl flashed across Escobar's face, causing Pat to think that if looks could kill Silvio's family would soon be calling for an undertaker. His associate had clearly told him both of them would be there. 'I only bring him when it is convenient,' Pat said by way of explanation. He looked around to his men, who had already sensed the unexpected change of mood. 'I wasn't expecting to see you,' he said, seeking to keep things light. 'It is a pleasant surprise. Why are you here?'

Escobar shrugged, still angry. 'Should I not be? Are there matters you only discuss with him?'

'Of course not. The only reason I am here is to help you.'

'Then why do I always feel like I am being played?' Pat looked to Silvio for assistance. This was odd. He was there to discuss future arrangements for cash collections. He couldn't think what might have happened to sour relations. He got only a blank face in response. 'What is wrong?'

'Always it is on your terms,' Escobar said. 'The collections, the deliveries . . . my son.'

So that was the issue.

'We all agreed it was best to limit the meetings to new year.

'. . . when it suits you,' Escobar said.

'When it suits Phillip. It is about his best interests.' Pat was trying hard to keep his voice level but mention of his son agitated him.

Escobar took a step forward and glowered up at the Englishman towering over him. 'From now on, you work for me – on my terms.'

Pat remained calm. How quickly they change, he thought. Just a few months ago this man was a nobody. Now he thought he could order anyone around. 'We always aim to please,' he said, with a tight smile.

As soon as they wrapped up their business Pat left the *finca*, thinking his next rendezvous with JB could not come soon enough. Surely, he would know what the hell was going on.

'What is the expression?' JB said, when they next met up at the Avenida de Las Américas. 'The king is dead. Long live the king.'

'The king?' Pat had said.

'Fabio Restrepo, the main cocaine dealer in Antioquia. The main dealer.'

'What happened?'

'Shot dead.'

'Who by?'

'Guess.'

Even allowing for what Pat already knew about Pablo Escobar, it still seemed shocking to hear what he was capable of. At least he knew why his dealings with Escobar had become harder. He asked his Panamanian colleague if he was sure the story was true.

JB shrugged. 'If not him, then someone on his orders. To be fair, there are a number of candidates. The Ochoa brothers – Fabio, Alonzo and Jorge. They were business partners but, instead of settling for a slice, they might have taken the whole pie. But you only have to look to see who's benefitted the most. Escobar. He's the main man in Paisa [the region that included several departments, among them Antioquia]. He controls the entire north-west of the country now. You're going to be busy.' Pat offered only a weak smile in response. He was already calculating the potential consequences. 'That's not all,' JB went on. 'According to my sources, within an hour of the murder Escobar called a meeting in a cantina on the outskirts of Rionegro. The location is significant: that's his turf. Apparently, he, Silvio and Gustavo met with the Ochoas and their hired hands and Escobar told them, "You work for me now."'

The same expression he'd used on me, Pat thought to himself.

'That no one challenged him or even made that much of a fuss tells its own story,' JB said. 'Restrepo's days were always numbered. It was just a case of who got there first. And Escobar probably knew the Ochoas didn't have his bottle. He probably justified the murder to himself and the rest of them. The end justified the means. When Escobar looked at Restrepo's operation he probably saw only obstacles, not opportunities. If he continued to feed into the existing model the end result would only by that Restrepo got richer at his expense. And he couldn't have that.'

'How good are your sources?' Pat said.

'Reliable informants.'

'I'll need to feed this back.'

'Of course,' JB said. 'There's something else they'll want to know too.'

What now? Pat thought.

'Escobar wants every smuggler to work for him. They're going to pool their resources and split the proceeds. They'll control supply and the price. He told them, "You side with me and I'll help keep you out of trouble."'

'And what was the response?'

'What could they say? They are all scared of him.'

'A cartel?' Pat said. 'For drug smugglers?'

JB nodded. 'The Medellín Cartel. You have to say, it has a certain ring to it, don't you think?'

Some weeks later Sir Arthur arrived in Colombia for his regular updates and his usual Saturday morning round of golf with Pat at the club. A lot had happened since his previous visit, although money was continuing to roll in from the *finca*.

'Something troubling you, old boy?' Sir Arthur said, once they'd stored away their clubs and changed out of their golf spikes.

'Why do you ask?' Pat said, knowing full well. Even Sir Arthur, who loved winning at anything, often at any cost, had spotted that Pat, a challenging opponent most of the time, had capitulated badly on the round of golf they'd played. It was uncharacteristic for him to lose by more than ten shots, as he just had. Something else must definitely be afoot.

'You seem a little preoccupied.'

Pat was not the type of person to air problems. He prided himself on being a solutions man. But now he bore the expression of someone who was troubled. Throughout his career, Pat had seen elements of Pablo Escobar's behaviour in others – it was what happened when someone got a little taste of power – but there was something about this individual that unnerved him. Was it the personal connection, Phillip, between them that made him feel this way? It was a question he would continually ask himself. Or was it the access they were granting him and the oil they were providing to grease the wheels of his operation that was feeding Escobar's inflated sense of importance? Or both?

But more than anything, it was their personal connection that continued to unsettle him. He felt it as his Achilles heel.

The boarding school arrangement helped enormously in terms of keeping Phillip safe, but it was when his son was back home in Colombia that he fretted. It didn't matter how much security he had, Pat always felt it was never enough. That was why he wanted his son with him when he made his trips to the *finca*. It wasn't an indulgence or reckless. It was a necessity. Pat knew he was the best person to protect his family. There had never been a tacit agreement with Escobar over access. Maybe it would have been better if there had been as, even without set rules, it still felt the Colombian was desperate to break them. The pressure he was exerting, coupled with the news from Medellín only added to Pat's unease.

Not all of this he could convey to Sir Arthur. To do so would be to admit weakness or that he was somehow not up to the job any more. That was the last thing he wanted. Judging by his performance on the course he obviously wasn't as good as hiding his feelings as he thought he was, however. And if there was an ideal forum at which to raise any niggling issues then over drinks on the patio of the Los Lagartos club was it.

'It's the operation,' Pat said after a moment's contemplation.

Sir Arthur instinctively took a glance around. 'Yes.'

'It's going well. We've established good connections in Medellín and Cali, the cash deliveries are bearing fruit and we're fulfilling our side of the bargain with our American friends.'

'And? Sounds like it's working out better than we ever hoped.'

'It is. On the business side of things, Gregorio has been extremely efficient. We are expanding our reach all the time. We have the president on side.'

'And a royal visit,' Sir Arthur interrupted. 'I know how much Gregorio was excited about that.

Pat smiled. He knew how much his boss also loved any endorsement from the royal family and the visit of the Queen's only daughter, Princess Anne, to Colombia and to De La Rue had been a very distinguished feather in the cap for Sir Arthur and Gregorio. If only the royal family knew of the business Sir Arthur and Pat had got themselves wrapped up in . . . They might not be so quick to give that side of the firm's business their stamp of approval.

'So, with all this positive news, why the long face?' Sir Arthur said.

'Well . . . ' Pat swirled the ice around in a glass of scotch. 'Maybe the operation is going too well.'

'How so?'

'The young Escobar.'

'Yes.'

'There's something about him.'

Sir Arthur sighed. Pat knew his boss hated vagueness but he was struggling to put his finger on what precisely troubled him. 'He wants the world . . . now.'

'No harm in a bit of ambition,' Sir Arthur said, taking a sip of his scotch. 'Where would we be but for a healthy dose?'

'Quite,' Pat said. 'But we didn't kill anyone to get here.'

'Not directly,' Sir Arthur said with a chuckle. Pat let the joke pass. 'Has this young chap actually done anyone in? I thought you said those were rumours.'

'I don't know,' Pat said. 'The more dealings I have with him the more I'm inclined to believe them. He seems to have no moral code. He's only just starting to see the fruits of his enterprises but already he's eliminating his competition.

'He's a criminal, for God's sake,' Sir Arthur spluttered. 'What do you expect?'

'Some honour amongst thieves?'

'This is Colombia, dear boy.'

'If we're not careful it could become the wild west again. More so. At the moment, his moves are purely financial but I wouldn't put it past him to spill more blood. And, if our intelligence is true, then once someone like that gets a taste for it . . . '

'It's a country in flux,' Sir Arthur said. 'You have to expect some lawlessness and, within that, some behaviours worse than others. What exactly is it about Escobar you don't like? You're not making this too personal, are you?'

Pat shook his head. 'I'm doing what's necessary, regarding that aspect.'

'True,' Sir Arthur nodded. 'It can't be easy where the boy is concerned but Escobar can't complain you're not keeping him informed of the lad's progress. What then?'

'I just think,' Pat looked in his glass, which was more in danger of becoming more melted ice than scotch and ginger ale, 'we have to watch this one.'

'Are we not doing that already?' Sir Arthur drained his glass. 'I sense you're not telling me the full story. Spit it out, for pity's sake.'

Pat finished his own drink and sat forward in his wicker chair. 'He's growing more powerful and generating more money than we ever foresaw. The money is rolling in like never before. He's running drugs in ever-increasing quantities into the US, mainly through Panama, and he has created a cartel to boost supply and maximise profits and power.'

Sir Arthur lounged back in his seat. 'Twas ever thus. It's what we do. We help build these characters up and, when the time comes, we pull the rug from under them. And, in the meantime, you need to butter this chap up, give him what he wants – to a certain extent. Make him feel important and convince him that you can do things for him that no one else can. Make yourself – and the firm – indispensable. Be more creative in your suggestions. Show him you can really help. And,' he added, while summoning a waiter for another round, 'we'll hope that at some point some little *chica* will come along to distract him with some children and take his mind off this world domination nonsense.'

Sir Arthur paused and regarded Pat. 'You don't seem convinced.'

Pat shook his head.

'What is it you fear with this Escobar?'

Pat sighed and sat forward in his chair. 'I fear we have created a monster.'

CHAPTER 23: THE HOUSES THAT PHILLIP BUILT

Pat recognised the tactic – he'd used it himself on others, many times. Arrange a meeting for a specific time but when your target arrives, keep them waiting. Make them stew. Let them know where the power lies in the relationship.

He sat, awaiting his audience with Pablo Escobar, and he knew he needed to be mindful of the gamesmanship; otherwise his blood would boil in the tropical heat of Medellín. That he had to jump through hoops for this hoodlum was bad enough. But it almost made him mad to think he was doing so when he was actually here to do him a favour. A huge one at that. Something that could set Escobar up for life.

Just remain calm, he told himself. Never let them see how annoyed you are. The young crime boss's time would come. But it would not be today.

'Señor Witcomb, sorry to have kept you waiting,' Escobar said, as he strode into the front room of the villa, accompanied by the ever-present Silvio. Pat bristled at the faux formality and the apology. He knew the Colombian wasn't the least bit regretful and he didn't have to look at his watch to know that nearly an hour had elapsed since he arrived. The hilltop ranch was a ghost town; a marked change from their previous visit, when heavily armed *sicarios* had squared off with his armed escort.

'Don't mention it. Time is not a concern for me,' Pat lied, keen to plough on without detour. He pulled out a document from his briefcase and unfolded it over the large wooden table. 'These are the plans Silvio would have told you about.' The only response he got was a disinterested shrug. Undeterred, he carried on. 'The Calatrava estate. A complex of luxury homes for only the very wealthy of Bogotá.'

'And why would I be interested in homes for rich people?'

'Because,' Pat said, 'you'd be making money from them.'

Now he had the attention he desired. The two men leaned over the table and looked at the blueprints for the development of high-end bungalows, villas and apartments in one of the most desirable areas of the capital. Pat did not mention that it was only three kilometres from Los Lagartos club. He did not want to give his business partners any ideas.

'Tell me how this works.'

Pat gave Escobar the same spiel he had previously given Silvio; real estate development invited funds from a wide range of investors: it would be almost impossible to determine the origin of his money, particularly as large amounts of clean cash would be coming from De La Rue's HQ with regard to a legitimate bank loan issued for the construction of the properties.

Escobar marvelled at the size of the properties and, at first, needed convincing that the majority were single houses, so large were the plots. It was a far cry from the slums of Medellín.

'In a way nothing changes,' Pat explained. 'The money still comes to me, is still processed by our firm, but it ends up in this building site. When the homes are sold the cash is returned, with profit. You could even think of it as funding the ordinary workers on the site. Thanks to your money they will be paid on time and not waiting on sales of the plots to further the development. This is just phase one of the complex. There are provisional plans to extend the site. When completed it will be one of the most desirable addresses in Colombia, which means the potential is there to keep investing and get a return for years.'

'You mentioned a bank loan,' Silvio said.

Pat explained that the loan was made by their mutual connection, Carlos Escobar. It would go to the construction company to begin the development and would be secured on their investment funds. Every dollar would be converted to pesos. Every peso would be accounted for. The profits accruing in the construction company's account, minus his commission and the loan repayments, could be withdrawn as legitimate, clean money.

'It is entirely up to you,' Pat went on, 'whether you keep this as your own investment, or involve your business partners – the others in your cartel.' The look on Escobar's face made Pat regret his choice of word immediately.

'What do you know of a cartel?' Escobar's eyes narrowed.

An awkward silence lengthened between them as Pat searched for the right thing to say. 'It is in our interests to keep abreast of any change in our clients' circumstances,' Pat said, smiling, trying to appear relaxed, even though he was suddenly aware of his heart racing. 'I'm sure you wouldn't expect anything less.'

Escobar looked to Silvio.

'I said nothing,' his associate said.

Pablo looked again at the plans. While he examined the drawings, he turned to Pat. 'Tell me, señor Witcomb, how can we be sure our conversations are private – with or without you being present?'

Pat inhaled deeply, conscious of Chalky's hidden device that he was sure was still running . . . and recording. 'You can be quite sure,' he said. 'It doesn't matter where in the world we operate, keeping secrets is the nature of our business as much as is making money.'

Escobar nodded to Silvio, who gestured to Pat to stand. 'You will understand our concern,' Silvio said. 'And our need to make sure that's the case.'

Pat hesitated and thought about protesting but, realising that might make him look guilty, stood up, his arms wide, awaiting the body search. 'Of course. It is not a problem.' He felt a trickle of sweat run down his spine. It was like someone had cranked up the heating and turned off the fan.

Silvio started wide at the palms and ran his hands along Pat's arms, feeling under his collar, patting the armpits that were now drenched with sweat. He pulled out the tie tucked into the shirt and examined the back. He ran his open hands down Pat's back and felt around his chest, running his fingers inside his waistband. He patted the pockets and then motioned to Pat to reveal their contents. Pat removed a wallet, which was examined. Pat then turned out the pockets. Silvio then ran his hands down the legs of Pat's trousers.

'Now the jacket,' Escobar said.

Pat winced as the chair scraped back over the stone floor. Silvio picked up the jacket and fished around in the pockets, removing the handkerchief in the top pocket. The outer pockets were still stitched closed. When he turned his attention to the inside pockets, Pat felt sure the sound of his heart would give the game away. It seemed to get louder the closer Silvio got. As the hand snaked into the inner pocket, Pat wondered how far he'd get if he made a dash for it. Would his bodyguards outside react quickly enough to rescue him? Would he be better smashing the heel of his hands into their faces before making his escape? His whole body tensed. This was it. Fight or flight.

Silvio's hand emerged empty. He looked for the other pocket on the opposite side and investigated there. 'Nothing,' he said, shrugging.

Escobar nodded. 'Thank you. You were saying?'

Pat tucked his tie back into his shirt and sat down, trying to regulate his breathing. How had Silvio not found it? He looked for any sign of a double-play, but the middleman's face gave nothing away. Regaining his composure, Pat continued: 'It is up to you if you want to share this opportunity with others. It might be beneficial to have some personal investments no one else knows about.'

Escobar continued to study the plans. 'You might be right. It troubles me it is only the wealthy who will benefit. It would be better if these were houses for the poor.'

Pat took the plans and folded them back up. It was time to leave on his own terms.

'I think, señor Escobar, that once you see the fruits of this endeavour you'll be able to build houses anywhere you like, for anyone you like.'

As soon as Pat was back in the car with his armed escort he searched in the pocket for the recording device. It wasn't there. He began to panic. Had it fallen out? Would it be found lying on the floor in the villa? Had Silvio found it and was he concealing the fact in order to blackmail Pat later? He searched the other pocket and patted the jacket down. There, at the bottom, inside the lining he could feel something small and round, like a coin. Further inspection of the inside pocket revealed a tear, just big enough for the recorder to slip through.

On the journey to the airport he reflected on his good fortune. He also reflected on what he had chosen not to tell Escobar or his cronies – that he had selected one of the bungalow plots on the Calatrava estate to his own family home. What better way to oversee the development of Escobar's investment? Another of the plots was going to Gregorio and his family. His De La Rue colleague would have to remain oblivious, though, to the source of large amounts of the funds going to the contractor. That would be another of Pat's little secrets.

CHAPTER 24: HOME SWEET HOME

When I returned home after another term at boarding school, Dad was excited about what he had to show me. With our customary escort we drove out towards Los Logartos but, before taking the usual turning, we headed towards a vast building site.

'It might not look like much,' Dad said, 'but that will be your new home.'

I'd already known, thanks to Mother's letters, that a move was in the offing. I stared at the construction site, but it was hard to comprehend what our house would look like when it was built. Dad said it would be big enough for Monique and me to each have our own en suite bathrooms and I started to come round to the idea. He said he'd chosen a bungalow because he wanted us all to be on one level. There were larger duplexes up the hill behind our plot.

I had with me my little box camera – I always took advantage of every opportunity to take photos. I called it my click-clack, because of the noise it made as I lowered the lever on the side to take a photo. The camera only took twelve-frame rolls and, as my shot selection left a little to be desired, I was regularly running out of film. Fortunately, Dad always seemed to have spare rolls and a black silk bag on him. Explaining the importance of not exposing the film to the light, he showed me how he changed a roll. He placed the camera and the replacement film roll into the bag, sealed up the bag by pulling on a drawstring and swapped out the films just by feeling his way around inside his clever portable dark room. I often got into trouble by taking photos of Dad while he was at work. I knew he didn't like pictures of him 'doing business' but the temptation was often far too great.

That day I took the first of several photos of the development before we returned to the house where he explained the plans and, as time went on and the house neared completion, he made every effort to make me feel involved. Despite his best efforts, for the next year, I felt in a state of flux. The thought of spending long holidays back in Colombia were what kept me going through the long terms at St Hugh's. Yet I felt I couldn't properly settle at home or in England, knowing that at some point we would be moving again. I was impatient for it to happen but slightly nervous about the potential upheaval. The longer I spent at boarding school the more I felt that my education was an unnecessary interruption to my exciting and somewhat privileged lifestyle in Colombia.

My mood wasn't improved by the prospect of having to sit common entrance exams. I detested school-work at the best of times but, knowing I now had to revise before the end of the term, I felt doubly depressed. Despite my gloom, I tried to make the most of the situation, throwing myself into the sport and outdoor activities that I loved. I enjoyed getting back into the rigorous rugby sessions and my outlook brightened even more when I made the cricket team. The school had its own Scout movement which I joined, loving our exercises in the woods and the life skills we learned. Our rugby coach, Mr Snow, was also the school's scout master and he must have seen some potential as, not long after I joined the Scouts, he promoted me to patrol leader. Things were looking up, but my joy turned out to be short-lived.

'Lights out' was the order for all pupils to be quiet and go to sleep. Even with the danger of frequent patrols, however, the risk to play up was sometimes overwhelming. A couple of the other boys started mucking about one night and I couldn't resist the temptation to join in. Of course, when the house master came around to find out what all the noise was about, the others had the sense to shut up and act all innocent. I was caught red-handed.

'You're coming with me,' he said gruffly, dragging me from the room while I vainly tried to protest my innocence.

I knew where we were heading – to Mr Young's study and the beating chair. The sadistic house master seemed to take great pleasure manhandling me into the semi-darkened room before ordering me to wait while he fetched the head teacher. Those moments, while I waited for my punishment, were almost as bad as the beating itself, as my mind filled with thoughts of how sore I would feel. Eventually Mr Young strode in, clearly annoyed at being disturbed after hours. He threw me a look of disgust and without a word picked up the large wooden brush. He motioned me towards the chair.

'Assume the position,' he said, almost in a whisper.

'Sir, I am very sorry . . . it was not like the housemaster told you. I was only —'

'Assume the position.' This time his words were so sharp and loud they shocked me into silence.

I bent over the chair, my hands on the arms. Through the darkness outside I could just make out the playing fields, where I longed to be – anywhere away from this room. It was at that moment that I cursed my choice of thin nightwear, wishing instead I had some special reinforced, padded pyjamas.

Whack!

The sound of the brush as it made contact was as violent as the pain that seared through me. I tried to yelp but the breath was jolted out of me. I barely had time to steady myself when the next blow came. Then the next. Then the next. I thought it would never end. Six blows in all, each more painful than the last. Finally, the punishment was over.

Or so I thought: 'For your insubordination you are hereby relieved of your duties as scout patrol leader and deselected from the cricket team until further notice.'

What? For making some noise after lights out? This was outrageous.

'Don't let it happen again,' he added before dismissing me back to my dorm.

I hobbled out of the room, the pain that still reverberated through my body mixing with rage and a sense of burning injustice. I returned to the stairs but, instead of heading up to my room, I stormed down to the door and outside. I picked up the biggest rock I could find and hurled it straight through the ancient, lead-lined, dining room window of the priceless Grade I-listed manor house.

Now I was for it.

The next set of lashings was longer but not half as painful, as I was buoyed by the satisfaction of sticking it to them through their fancy window. I figured there was no way the school could punish me any more as they had already denied me the activities I loved.

However, Dad found out what I'd been up when a sternly worded letter accompanied by a rather large bill found its way over the Atlantic to the company's headquarters. Luckily for us both, Gregorio stepped in to settle the bill. I hoped that by the time I returned for Easter the matter would have been forgotten about. I was wrong.

'You need to learn to control that temper,' he said. 'You've not got it from your mother or me. If you want to make it in the world, control it – or it will get you into more trouble and your godfather might not be around to bail you out next time.'

I had no idea where that temper came from or when it would erupt. Sometimes it would just fire up and the strength of it shocked me. I knew Dad was right. If I didn't get a handle on it soon who knew what damage I might cause?

With Dad's words ringing in my ears, I arrived back in England for the summer term. I imagined I'd return home in the summer to a period of upheaval. With fewer distractions, I belatedly settled down to the job in hand and studied for the entrance exams. With so much work to get through, the term dragged but, eventually, it was time to return to Colombia for the long summer holiday. When Dad and his team picked me up from the airport I was already in a state of excitement – but it would soon reach new heights.

'We have a surprise for you,' he said. 'We're going to our new home in the Calatrava estate.'

The home that I had been desperate to see completed was right there in front of me. I could hardly believe it. As Dad had said, it was considerably larger than our previous accommodation. Monique and I did indeed each have our own en suite bathrooms and our bedrooms had their own patio doors leading out to landscaped grounds that were meticulously maintained by the gardeners. Otilia's living quarters were set apart from us, behind the kitchen, with a little private eating area and a yard of her own. It was strange but comforting to see all our possessions rearranged in our new home.

Until the estate's guardhouse was completed, we had a temporary structure on the front drive. It was a small box with a stool squeezed inside and looked like it was made of tin, as it shone in the sunlight. It reminded me of the huts used by guards at Buckingham Palace to shelter from rain, only ours had been unceremoniously dumped on an uneven bit of concrete and its door didn't fully close. The little house would sway and rock every time the guard sneaked in to have a cigarette or a nap and I would sometimes sneak up behind the front door and slowly open it. The creaking sound would make the guard jump up and the sight of him bursting out of his tin shed, trying not to look as if he had been having a little rest, was a great source of amusement for my friends. The guards yearned for the night shift, when they would at least be safe from schoolboy pranks, as we were always dreaming up new ones to play on them. I particularly enjoyed creeping up behind the hut as if we were on some kind of military exercise, banging on the back and running off.

The arrival of two huge, fierce Alsatian guard dogs soon put an end to our high-jinks. They were the first sign of De La Rue's efforts to raise the visible level of security, both at our house and at Gregorio's. My godfather took the older, fully trained dog and we had the younger one, which still had some way to go before it learned how to deter strangers from approaching the house. I liked its friendly nature and looked forward to saying 'Hello' to it in the evening before getting ready for bed.

The dogs weren't just for our benefit. They also represented a foray into a new business sector, the long-term plan being that De La Rue would offer personal security to the elite of Bogotá. Although we didn't appreciate it at the time, we were clearly the guinea pigs, providing real-life scenario training for the guards and their newly acquired canine companions. Every evening a changing of the guard took place. I was always intrigued at the sight of them passing the revolver and belt of ammunition, but each gun was registered to a particular house and not to the guards. Regular as clockwork, a new team would roll up in the De La Rue truck to relieve their colleagues every six hours. It became a comforting part of our daily life.

Our new home was also fitted with an alarm. I heard it once, during a test the electricians carried out when they installed it. The sound was deafening, so loud you couldn't think. It sounded like those air-raid sirens in the old black-and-white war movies I had seen at May's house in Swiss Cottage. If it ever went off for real it would wake the whole neighbourhood which was, of course, the idea. The large, orange klaxon speaker had been placed in the kitchen near the maid's quarters. Dad said that any intruders would be so startled and disorientated by the racket that they would be easy for the guards to apprehend. Once I heard it at work for myself I understood how anyone would be sent into a state of confusion.

Dad called the estate 'The houses that Phillip built' and even had a special plaque engraved with those words. This was screwed to a wooden block that had been carved out of one of the large, wooden, roof support beams. I used it as a doorstop in my bedroom. He said that he credited me with enabling the close relationship with Gregorio. It was through this that De La Rue had become a success and that all of this development work had become possible. It would be years later that I discovered the real reason – that the construction of this vast estate, along with many others, was funded entirely from dollars that had been personally entrusted to him by my real father.

De La Rue sent our young dog to an intensive training camp and supplied a replacement for the two weeks that it was away. Upon hearing the truck pull up on the drive, I adopted my usual observation post – the dining room window ledge. I watched as the new guard announced his arrival by opening the back of the truck to reveal an Alsatian that was easily twice the size of ours, restrained by a thick metal chain. Immediately, I sensed that this animal was not going to appreciate my usual evening greeting. It looked like it would tear my arm off before I had a chance to say, 'Hello.'

The guard tied the beast to a post next to his hut and then came to the door to speak to Dad. Dad then made a general announcement to family and staff alike. 'For the next two weeks the new dog outside will be released into our garden every evening to look after us and make sure no one can get into the house. The only issue is that it has not been trained to distinguish between any bad guys and us. It is trained to attack anyone not wearing the De La Rue uniform.'

'What? So anyone else is just dinner?' I asked.

'Pretty much,' Dad said.

Otilia's new job was to secure all the doors and windows at six every evening. Mother was a bit put out by the new arrangement, as she would now have to wait at least half an hour for the 6 p.m. drinks trolley to arrive in the sitting room. An exception to this rule was made when we entertained guests at the house, which happened at least twice a week. On these occasions, the dog was tethered to the post on the drive. The dog quickly became a main topic of conversation whenever we had dinner parties. We often hosted visiting dignitaries from London who were much more used to commuting to a leafy part of the home counties of England rather than the wild west of Bogotá. Yet our unnamed, newly acquired deterrent never barked; the dog merely rumbled out a menacing growl that left staff, family and guests under no illusions as to its intentions if left to its own devices.

We pitied the fool who tried to get past the dog to break into the house and assumed its presence would be more than enough to deter any would-be intruder. We were wrong.

CHAPTER 25: SILVER OR LEAD

Meanwhile, over in Medellín, it was beginning to look like Sir Arthur had been right about one thing. A woman had come along and turned Pablo Escobar's head.

History repeated itself when Maria Victoria Henao Vellejo first caught Escobar's eye. She shared the same first name as Maria Sendoya, the girl caught in the crossfire in the *finca*. And, like that ill-fated former lover, Maria Vellejo was under the age of consent when she met Escobar. She was just twelve and he twenty-three when she first saw him riding his motorbike. Escobar bided his time, using a go-between to let Maria know he was interested until she turned thirteen, when he began pursuing her in earnest.

Maria knew nothing of his drug smuggling but was captivated by this man who drove flash cars and splashed money on rings and nights out, while seemingly not working. They had a volatile relationship and she was acting against her family's wishes, but Maria fell for him when Escobar professed undying love. Like many people in his life, she was powerless to say, 'No' and, even though he cheated on her repeatedly and disappeared for weeks on end, when she was fifteen they ran off to get married. On 29 March 1976, ignoring last-ditch appeals from her family, Maria and Pablo were married. She went to school while he went off to 'work' – at what, she did not know.

Just two months later, she got the shock of her life when he was arrested, along with Gustavo and another associate. They were caught with 26 kilograms of coca paste, hidden in a spare tyre as they returned to Medellín from Ecuador. Escobar tried unsuccessfully to bribe the judge and then hired his brother to represent him, suspecting that the conflict of interest would prompt the judge to step down. He duly did and the replacement was more amenable to bribes. In a further stroke of luck for Escobar, the two drug agents who arrested him were found dead. According to folklore, the case established a rule Escobar would live by from then on – *plata o plomo* (silver or lead). If someone could not be bought then they would receive a bullet.

Having escaped justice, Escobar's business boomed. Demand from the USA for cocaine was seemingly insatiable. The more his cartel could ship, the more dollars flooded in. One cheque alone was apparently made out for over three million dollars. And that was just in the early days. This was where Sir Arthur's prediction failed. Getting the woman of his dreams did not, it seem, distract Escobar enough to take his eye off his criminal enterprise.

He had a wife, more wealth than he had previously imagined and complete power over his empire. There was only one thing missing . . .

CHAPTER 26: BLOODSHED

After a week in our new home with our temporary guard dog on patrol, I was getting into a routine. Each night, as I settled down in my bed to a good read, I could hear the comforting sounds of the guard talking to Otilia, letting her know he was about to release the beast to carry out its patrol round the garden.

Hearing the heavy breathing as it sniffed out its territory under my bedroom window helped to nurture feelings of security. Dad had really got this right. Our new home and my bedroom were comfortable and felt safe. I couldn't wait to immerse myself in Edgar Rice Burroughs' *New Adventures of Tarzan*. Reading his books gave me an escape from the real world. Without television, this was the best way to travel into adventure-land. Favourite books came and went, such as *Reach For The Sky*, the story of the wartime flying ace Douglas Bader, but I always had a soft spot for the jungles of Africa and the adventures of Tarzan. A book lasted much longer for me than it did for my parents. I still hadn't fully mastered English, which had a much more extensive and complex vocabulary than the South American Spanish I had grown up with. Invariably, I dropped off to sleep just before an exciting bit, which meant I had to read the whole chapter again the next night to get the gist of it.

I was reading another gripping Tarzan story, one night, how he'd just managed to see off some raiding party of native cannibals, when I must have dozed off. I woke with a shock to the ear-piercing sound of the air-raid-style siren alarm. Trying to regain my senses, I could hear Otilia shouting. My room was in darkness and her incomprehensible screams startled and confused me further. I leaped out of bed just as I caught sight of a dim torchlight shining through the doorway that led straight onto the garden. The door had been opened. Was that what had triggered the alarm?

I suddenly thought of the fierce dog off the leash and, frightened out of my wits, I ran for the door that led to the hallway and Dad's room. I didn't make it. The rough hand of a man gripped me firmly round my neck. I panicked, but instead of fighting my way clear I froze. I caught a strong, grimy stench of alcohol and tobacco. The callused hand pulled me backwards and now a thick arm pinned me back against a broad chest. I tried to scream but all that came was a pathetic yelp. A large hand went over my mouth and, for a moment, I couldn't breathe. The attacker shoved me against the wall next to the door, knocking the wind from me. I prayed that someone would hear, although I could barely hear anything at all above the din of the siren.

I stood, petrified, as the intruder kept me up against the wall while he turned and scanned the room with his flashlight. To the right was the door leading to the hall, opposite the route to the garden. As the torch locked on the open doorway it illuminated two green eyes. It was the guard dog! I gasped, now even more terrified. Its huge body nearly filled the doorframe and its teeth were bared.

I felt my attacker's hold loosen, as he clearly weighed up his options. Whatever his original intent it now seemed to come second to self-preservation. Amid the din I could hear a guard shout. The dog remained stock-still. More shouting came from within the house. It was chaos.

The man moved towards the doorway, pushing me in front. I seized the chance to break free from his grasp and scrambled over the bed. The intruder ran to the garden door and somehow managed to kick his way past the dog and, jumping up on a fence next to the house, then made it up and on the low, sloping roof above my bedroom.

The alarm suddenly stopped but the sound of mayhem continued. Frozen with fear in the darkness and not knowing whether to run or sit still, I listened to the fearsome barking of the dog and the muffled thudding of the intruder's feet above my head, dislodging tiles that came smashing to the ground just by the door.

The sight of a figure made me jump once more but fright turned to relief when I saw it was Barandiga, torchlight in one hand, revolver in the other. 'OK?' he shouted. I nodded. He closed the door and focused again on the man I could still hear scrambling up the roof.

Feeling a little braver, I went to the window. Even though we were separated by glass, the presence of the dog, barking manically, teeth still bared, just feet below my window was terrifying to behold. Barandiga had his torch trained on the roof, gun raised. He was shouting almost as frantically.

I could hear the wail of approaching sirens. The sound of our alarm had triggered a response from military police in barracks located not far from the estate. The sky was ablaze with the reflection of flashing blue lights as more men streamed into the garden. Before any of them could get into position I saw Barandiga take aim again. He shouted something and then fired. Instinctively, I ducked but remained peering over the window ledge. Two more shots rang out. A body fell past my window and landed with a dull thud on the ground. The dog leapt forward and sunk its teeth into an arm for good measure. The intruder was beyond struggling.

'Phillip!'

I jumped again. It was Dad, bursting into my room from the hallway.

'Are you OK?' Dad asked. He pulled me away from the window and smothered me, shielding me from the events outside. It was too late though. Those images would join the other violent episodes stored in my memory banks to be replayed when I least wanted them. The whole incident had lasted seconds but, as I replayed the trauma over in my mind, it seemed to go on forever.

Dad took me into the room my parents shared and fussed over me, checking that I was not hurt and wanting to know what happened. When the intruder opened my door it must have set off the alarm and he was dismayed that the rest of the security had seemingly been so easily breached.

Dawn brought with it some relief. An air of calm descended which seemed unthinkable just a few hours earlier. By the time the sun rose the intruder's body had been removed and a blanket placed over the blood spilled on the grass. The mood was understandably sombre until Monique shattered the gloom and surprised us all by emerging from her bedroom, asking Dad why there was a blanket in the garden. Amazingly, she had slept through it all.

Seemingly endless rounds of visits from doctors and psychiatrists consumed the next few days, as they all tried to assess whether or not I would be permanently traumatised. An army colonel was put in charge of the investigation, as there was little faith in the local police. Having a senior officer at the house also meant that we would be surrounded by army trucks and soldiers until they'd found who was responsible. Dad must have hated all the fuss; he always preferred to keep a low profile. As I did whenever I felt under stress, I retreated to my sketchbook to draw, which helped to dispel my anxiety. Dad and the colonel chatted to me while I drew pictures, subtly trying to coax additional information out of me about the attacker.

The following day the colonel arrived at the house, beaming. He announced to Dad that they had caught the gang responsible. Some of his soldiers had come across a group of men sitting in a car just up the road from the house. They detained them and, after interrogation, the men had confessed. The investigation was scaled down after that, but the colonel remained a regular visitor to the house, keeping Dad updated and exchanging information.

He turned up off-duty one evening with his wife. It was the first time I had seen this man in civilian clothing. It was hard to believe the smartly dressed gentleman sat in front of me, relaxing with a glass of whisky, was the same man I had seen a day before in uniform, wearing a holstered side-arm. Even more interesting was that I now recognised this colonel as someone I had seen in one of our regular visits to Medellín. He had often sat with the group of men at the centre-front table and seemed to know the individual who had taken such an interest in me. From the snippets of conversation I overheard while he chatted to Dad, it seemed he was normally based in Medellín where he had been on the trail of members of a gang. It seemed a strange coincidence that he would now be here. Did that group of men have something to do with the man who broke into my room attempting to take me?

In the weeks that followed, the atmosphere in the house returned to normal. The proper guard hut was completed and the security presence around the house was beefed up. Our own dog returned, giving us the reassurance that at least it could distinguish us from any would-be attacker. For me, though, the house was never really the same again. It had gone from being our own little oasis, a paradise away from the mean streets of Bogotá, to being yet another location where terror had visited. Why did they always seem to come for me? Was I just unlucky? Were they opportunistic thugs targeting a rich family or did they know who I was? And if they tried once, would they come again?

Such thoughts meant my nights were disturbed for a significant time afterwards. I didn't just have nightmares about being snatched but had other visions too; that woman in red crying in pain, people grabbing me, a feeling that someone was always chasing me. My parents did their best to reassure me we were safe now. They blamed the attack on the turbulent times we were living through and the lawlessness that had gripped large elements of the population. It would settle down, they promised.

I wanted to believe them but I couldn't stop thinking that once again Barandiga had saved me – from what, though, I wasn't entirely sure. As I prepared to go back to England and to school, at least I knew that as long as he was around I was safe.

*

The imposing building seemed to me like Colditz Castle, as described in the story of Douglas Bader. Its red walls rose before me. A sign outside might as well have read, 'Abandon hope all ye who enter here.' Instead it said, '*Floreat Luctona*', which I later learned meant 'May Lucton flourish'.

We were at Lucton School in rural Herefordshire. I had passed the entrance exams and this would be my new home whenever I was in England, once the registration was completed and I'd finished my last term at St Hugh's. This visit, made with my parents, was to get a feel for the place where I'd see out the remaining years of my education.

We met with the headmaster Keith Vivian, a large man with huge, shovel hands. He towered over me and told me, somewhat unconvincingly, how happy I would be there. As we wandered around the grounds, I had a deep sense of foreboding. I thought it might be nerves I was feeling about going to a new place where, once again I'd be fighting to keep pace with other boys who were really three years older than me. I couldn't quite put my finger on it though. I just had a sense that something bad was going to happen.

CHAPTER 27: THE ASSASSINATION

When the news of the failure of the attempt to take Phillip filtered back to Medellín, one man must have been furious. Not only had the would-be kidnappers failed in their objective but the collateral damage was massive; one dead, three others in custody.

They had not gone for half-measures in this attack. Apparently, all those on the mission were trusted *sicarios*. Pablo Escobar had known the kidnapper killed by Barandiga for years; he knew the man's mother. The pain Escobar himself must have felt would have gone way beyond his frustration at a job gone wrong. The others he didn't know as well and, although he was probably confident they wouldn't give too much away about who was behind the mission, he wouldn't have been thinking of the personal cost. He would have been thinking about retribution. This would not be allowed to pass. This death would be avenged – and quickly.

By the time Pat found out about Escobar's reaction it was too late to stop the devastating repercussions. An opportunity for revenge came even sooner than Escobar expected. When he was told about the plan, he thought it sounded perfect. Not only would he be able to take a hit at the very person who must have infuriated him the most at that moment – Pat Witcomb – and remind him exactly who held the power in their special relationship, but he was also given a chance to remove a very stubborn obstacle standing in the way of his ambition. Above all, however, this opportunity presented the possibility of vengeance for the death of a loyal companion. With one meticulously planned attack, Escobar would be able to strike fear into the organisation that he must have thought had taken too many liberties. He would show them that they weren't the only ones with spies and connections.

When Silvio explained how it would play out, Escobar loved what he heard. According to intelligence their target was going to be in a particular armoured truck and they knew the job and the time. The intended route, which changed daily, would only be confirmed on the morning of the cash collection. However, their informant told them that the trucks almost always passed one particular junction next to a railway crossing. An ambush had a high chance of success.

A team was sent ahead to ensure there were no cock-ups. They had positioned themselves early and, leaving nothing to chance, another member of the team was posted on the gate of the headquarters at Avenida de Las Américas. They confirmed the truck had left on time and was headed in the direction that matched their intelligence.

Using walkie-talkies, the lookouts kept in contact as, at 8 a.m., the first of the trucks rumbled out of the security gates. At first it seemed as if the conspirators might have to abandon their plan as the vehicle did not take the direction they had expected. Had De La Rue been tipped off? Had another change been made in addition to the one already implemented that morning? The lookout on the gate jumped on his scooter and tailed the truck, being careful not to be spotted. All was as they had hoped. After a short detour, the truck rejoined its scheduled route. The biker raced ahead to make sure the vehicle did indeed reach its intended pick-up. Once the bags of cash were loaded, the biker ensured the truck followed the route indicated via their intelligence. Once he was satisfied there would be no further complications, the biker radioed in his confirmation. It was on.

The men on the junction did not have to wait long. In under ten minutes the truck came into view. Just then, a school bus pulled up just beyond the junction, at the precise spot they needed the truck to be. The three men desperately debated what to do. Their instructions had been to keep it clean. No one would have wanted to inform the boss about collateral damage or, worse, a change of plan. Running out to tell the driver to move – revealing their hand in the process – was not an option. The truck trundled closer. They conceded they would have to let it pass. The vehicle came to a halt. At first, the men didn't understand what was happening. Then they realised. The driver was letting the school bus pull out. The small gesture of courtesy would be his last act of kindness.

With the bus gone, the junction was clear of traffic and the truck edged forward.

The explosion echoed around the streets. The truck rose into the air and bounced once before coming to rest on its side, its security doors hanging open. There was no time to sit back and admire their handiwork. The men's instructions had been clear: 'Take everything. They have stolen from me. I will steal from them.' Two of the men donned motorcyclist helmets and ran forward and the third member of the team backed the van up to be nearer to the truck. A small group of onlookers began to gather round as the men loaded three bags of cash. Once that task was complete, one of the men ran to the front of the vehicle. To gasps of people staring from the roadside, he fired two shots through the windscreen, just to make sure.

*

Pat could scarcely believe it when Gregorio broke the news. He had not expected such a brazen and vindictive act. When he heard who had been targeted in the truck, his shock turned to anguish, not just for the victims and their families but for Phillip. How would he explain this to his already traumatised son?

His devastation quickly gave way to anger. He knew exactly who was behind the senseless act of violence, and why. He wanted to fly to Medellín confront the man and have a bullet put through his skull. Which was why Sir Arthur, on hearing what had happened, said he was going to fly out immediately. A powder keg was threatening to explode. He must have feared that seventeen years of hard work would be lost if he didn't defuse the situation – and fast.

*

I was at school in England at the time that Pablo Escobar dramatically broke the uneasy truce that had existed between my father and him, although I knew nothing of what was going on back in Colombia. I was still at St Hugh's, although it felt strange to have to be there when I knew I would be soon moving on. If I'd found it difficult to concentrate before it was even doubly difficult. Although the kidnap attempt on our estate had terrified me, the longer I spent away from home the more I missed it. I counted the days until I could see everyone again. By the time the autumn term ended and I boarded the flight home I was excited to get re-acquainted with my friends and family.

We crossed the Atlantic without any problem but as soon as we touched down in Bogotá I could sense something wasn't right. Dad came to meet me in the Chevrolet as usual. Martinez was driving and there was the Jeep with the armed escort. Dad greeted me with a smile and a warm embrace that felt tighter than his normal hug.

'Where's Barandiga?' I said, climbing into the car and noticing my bodyguard was absent. I could tell by the look on Dad's face that something terrible had happened. His mouth moved but no words came out. For the first time in my life I thought I was about to see him cry.

'I'm sorry son,' he said eventually. 'Barandiga's gone.'

'Gone? Where? He wouldn't leave me.' Tears were already streaming down my face as I demanded answers, even though deep inside I knew what Dad was going to tell me.

'There was an incident. One of our trucks was attacked. He didn't survive. I'm so sorry. We're all so sad.'

'An attack? When? Why was he on the truck? He's meant to be protecting me.'

My whole body lurched into deep sobs. I couldn't breathe. Barandiga was my friend. He had twice saved me from being abducted. This wasn't happening. It surely wasn't true.

'I know, but with you not here, his job was on the trucks. He was our best man – but he didn't stand a chance. It was not fair.'

I couldn't take any more information. I cried for the duration of the journey home. I got out of the car still half-expecting him to be standing there, waiting on me. He had been a constant presence by my side whenever I was in Colombia. I tried to think of the last conversation we'd had, before we left for England. It seemed so long ago and I cursed myself for not being able to remember the details. If I'd known it would be the last time, I would have said more, hugged him tighter. When I calmed down Dad explained that his funeral was still to be held, so I would be able to go and pay my respects. That gave me some comfort at least.

I felt miserable for days, although in itself that wasn't an unusual sensation for me whenever I first arrived back from England. It always took me a few days to acclimatise and get over the altitude sickness I suffered at nearly 9,000 feet above sea level. I'm not sure if my sickness was worse on that occasion or whether it was a culmination of the grief and trauma I had suffered. Thankfully, I improved a little on the morning of Barandiga's funeral. I wanted to have a clear head for his send off.

De La Rue had made the arrangements for a small church to be used at the end of a road in central Bogotá. There was a large turnout, including senior figures from the company, like Sir Arthur – who had extended his stay – Gregorio and the other British and Colombian executives. This was my first experience of death and of a funeral. I found the service poignant and moving. I would never forget the man who put my safety above his own.

Dad always kept a lid on his emotions but he had been particularly quiet since I'd returned home. I saw him and Sir Arthur locked in deep conversations before the funeral and when the formalities were over they resumed their discussions.

I didn't know it but our future life in Colombia was on the line.

CHAPTER 28: VENDETTA

Pat resented the position in which he found himself. He had given everything to further De La Rue's secret operation, but for what? When he'd signed up he did not realise his job was to create a tyrant, put his son in danger and cost the lives of people who worked for him.

Sir Arthur had been doing everything in his power to calm him down, to try and impress upon him the bigger picture. Pat could see the big picture. He could see how this would end – and it wouldn't be pretty. Escobar would, of course, deny all involvement. Pat could almost hear him: this is Colombia – when you are in the cash transportation business you are a target for thieves.

'But,' Pat told Sir Arthur, 'this was not a robbery. It was an assassination. Barandiga had been defending Phillip and had been involved with killing Escobar's *sicarios*. This was Escobar telling us that we are going to die for killing his people. He is mounting a vendetta. He's letting us know that this is how he will deal with things if they are not going his way. You can't stop us, he is saying, if we want to demonstrate our authority.'

Sir Arthur listened to the analysis and sympathised greatly but his job was to keep his employee focused and Pat knew it. And Sir Arthur had his own take on what was happening that made it more a symptom of the company's success.

'It's a natural reaction,' Sir Arthur said, 'not getting his own way. It shows we have him by the balls. I imagine working with us infuriates him. You have his son yet he is relying on you to help him move his money. It's a dangerous tightrope you are both walking. He probably views you in the same light as you view him. You are a kidnapper in his eyes. You are only handling his money as a favour, as a sop and one day we all might be gone and where would that leave him? He is pushing back and perhaps understandably so. We just have to keep calm heads. You are due to see him in Medellín at the end of the year as usual. Go, be yourself and give nothing away. Never let him see how much this is affecting you.'

Pat could hear what his boss was saying but he'd thought long and rationally about what he wanted to do. The attack on the armoured car, coming so soon after the latest kidnap attempt, was the last straw. He told Sir Arthur in no uncertain terms. He would continue to do the De La Rue's work – but only on the condition he moved us all out of harm's way . . . for good.

CHAPTER 29: LEAVING

The first sense I got that something was up was hearing Dad speaking on the phone. He never raised his voice to anyone, no matter the circumstances, but here he was – shouting. I wasn't sure to whom he was speaking at first.

'I know what's best for my son,' he said. 'His home is wherever we are.' There was a pause before he signed off by saying, 'You do that.'

The next thing I knew Gregorio was at the door. He was even angrier than Dad had been. Clearly this was a continuation of their heated phone call. My godfather was a naturally more emotive man than my dad but this was a side to him I had never seen before. 'You can't take Phillip with you,' he yelled.

'I will do whatever I think best,' Dad responded. I thought they were discussing the annual trip to Medellín, on which Dad and I were about to embark. Quickly, it became apparent there was something more permanent in the offing. 'I have no choice,' Dad said. 'Like I told you my job is moving and it's better if we all move.'

'Phillip's home is in Colombia,' Gregorio raged. 'Go and do Arthur's bidding but leave my godson here.'

They were going at it hammer and tongs. Mother then waded in: 'Gregorio, with all due respect, this is a family matter.'

That was like a red rag to a bull. In Colombia the role of godfather is taken very seriously. He had been a huge presence in my life for as long as I could remember. To him I *was* family.

I could only sit there silently watching the people who cared for me tear into each other. I'm not sure they even noticed I was listening to their every word. They went at it for quite some time. It ended with Gregorio storming out. The argument clearly upset Dad as he fixed himself a drink and made it clear he wanted to be alone. Later, he came to sit with me in my room and explained what was going on.

He was under orders from Sir Arthur to set up an office of De La Rue in Santo Domingo, the capital of the Dominican Republic, an island in the Caribbean about a three-hour flight away.

'What, and we would be moving house?' I said.

'I'm afraid so. It makes sense to live there while I'm working,' he said.

'But what about our life here?' I said, thinking of the friends I'd miss and the lifestyle I enjoyed.

'Colombia is not the place it was,' Dad said solemnly. 'There is a lot of trouble. It could be years before it settles down. It will be safer for us all if we move.'

He distracted me by telling me what our new home might be like. He had been eyeing up a penthouse apartment that overlooked a beautiful park. 'And, we might even be able to rent a beach house in Boca Chica, by the sea. You'll love it.'

That sounded cool. My mind started to wander, lost in the possibilities of hanging at the beach all summer long. 'Do I still have to go to boarding school?' I asked, hopefully.

'I'm afraid so,' he laughed. 'There's no getting out of that.'

The move would be organised while I was away at boarding school. I was due to start at Lucton after the Christmas holidays. It was an odd time to be joining, midway through the school year, but I just had to accept it. Dad told me that he and I would first be travelling to Medellín for the annual new year party. I had grown more comfortable with the annual event, but I still considered it a little strange and, more than anything, quite dull. The upside, though, was that it was going to be just Dad and me. During those long stretches away at boarding school I missed him terribly and relished the chance to be with him, even if I knew for large chunks of the time he might be distracted with business. That also wasn't bad as, in my mind, it might mean a helicopter or armoured car ride.

Beforehand, though, I sensed Dad was not quite himself. He seemed withdrawn and quieter than usual. I got the feeling he didn't want to be there – neither in Medellín nor the party. I was similarly downcast. Not having Barandiga by my side made me feel slightly nervous, even though we had Martinez and a security escort. I was right to feel apprehensive. As soon as we entered the huge ballroom it felt like we were entering a different world. I had to double-check we were in the same place. The party was in full swing, there was music playing and the atmosphere was raucous. The group of men at the front of the room was so much bigger than previous years. There were women hanging off them and I could see guns on display, either stuffed into waistbands or being waved around. The air felt charged with danger.

Dad pulled me close to him. 'We won't stay long.'

He guided me through the throng to where I saw Silvio sitting. Even he looked different, more at one with the ruffians around him than the smartly dressed business associate of Dad's I'd known before. As we approached, I saw him tap the back of a man standing beside him. He turned and I recognised the man. It was don Pablo. He faced us but it was as though he looked through us. His eyes were blank and his face expressionless. Then, after a moment, there was a hint of a smile.

'You came. And you brought him. I didn't think you would.'

'I always honour my side of the bargain,' Dad said.

To me, Escobar said: 'How are you? I heard there was some trouble at your house.'

I could feel Dad tense next to me. His grip on my shoulder was a little firmer.

I shrugged. He hadn't said it in a very sympathetic way. It was almost mocking. His tone and the noise of the room made me feel uncomfortable. I suddenly missed Barandiga more than ever. Something about the sight of the men around us reminded me of the incidents at the Calatrava and at our old house.

Escobar looked as though he was going to say something else but thought better of it. He continued to look in my direction but I had the feeling I wasn't even registering with him. It was like his mind was somewhere else. Finally, he looked at Dad. 'And the other side of your bargain?'

'The arrangements are as we agreed?'

Escobar nodded.

'Then I will see you there,' Dad said, looking around the room. We stood out in this crowd, our smart attire and attitude in stark contrast to the sea of open shirts and loutish behaviour, and we were attracting attention. 'I trust you won't be offended if we don't stay for the festivities,' he added.

Escobar just shrugged.

Dad gave a nod of his head and directed me away. On the way out of the hotel he remained in his reserved mood, only offering one-word answers to my many questions.

'At least we won't have to do that again,' he said, as Martinez opened the door to our car.

The following morning, we arrived at Medellín airport and drove straight on to the tarmac towards a little Avianca jet, of the type that had brought us here. Suddenly the car turned away from the jet and headed towards an older aircraft that was parked up at the end of the taxiway near the grass verge. This Douglas DC-4 plane had propeller engines mounted on the wing and looked like one of the

Second World War model aircraft that I had hanging from the ceiling of my bedroom. A cabin crew member was waiting at the top of a set of rickety stairs. Dad showed me on to the steps and told Martinez to take me up to find our seats at the front. He was going to wait on the tarmac for a few minutes with the uniformed officers.

I peered down through my window and was surprised to see the man from the night before, don Pablo, talking to Dad. A number of jeeps surrounded them on the tarmac, filled with the same group of gun-toting men who had been at the ballroom with Pablo. While Dad and Escobar talked, the other men were handing large black bags over to the uniformed officers. With my nose pushed up against the round window of our DC-4 I could see the handover quite clearly.

Once the bags were loaded onto the aircraft Dad shook hands with the man and boarded up the steps with his officers. I expected other passengers would now be allowed to join us but it turned out we were the only ones. Usually the short hop over the Andes took forty minutes but as this was an older plane it was going to take an hour longer.

'What is the deal with that man?' I asked Dad once we were airborne.

He sighed. 'He's just a business partner.'

'Not one you enjoy dealing with?' I said.

He looked at me and half-smiled.

'You could say that.'

'What was in all those bags?'

'Money,' Dad said. 'We process his money like we do our other clients.'

I thought about that for a while. 'Then he should be a bit nicer to you,' I said. 'It looks like you're helping him get rich.'

Dad chuckled. 'You would think. But the good thing is we don't have to bother about him or Medellín any more. Once we move to Santo Domingo it will be a new start for us all.'

'But I'll miss my friends,' I said.

'And I'm sorry about that but they can come and visit. And think of how much fun it will be to take them around the city, or along the beach front in a chauffeur-driven car; things that are impossible to do here because of the trouble.'

That did sound like fun. Maybe Santo Domingo would be good. I could see a downside though. 'Will there be any more trips on a helicopter with you for work?'

Dad thought about this for a moment. 'Perhaps not but I'll still be doing the same job as I do in Colombia, so you can come along with me when you're home for the holidays. And, do you know what? In the Dominican Republic I'll have the use of a small Cessna plane. You can come on that. I think you'll like it.'

It was the most animated I had seen my dad in weeks – since the raid on the house, in fact. Maybe he was right. Perhaps moving away from Colombia would be good for us. I had to admit that one aspect of life in England that I appreciated was not having twenty-four-hour security following my every step. Would it be possible to have a home where I didn't need protection? If so, that was worth doing . . . especially when bodyguards could get killed.

As we settled into the flight, Dad and I chatted more about what the move would be like and what the houses would be like in the new country. The more we talked the more I came around to the idea. Dad made it sound exciting. It would be sad to leave Gregorio and the various 'uncles' who had helped look after me all these years but he was right, Colombia was becoming a violent, dangerous place. If Dad didn't want to be a part of it then maybe it was time to leave.

The old plane rattled all the way back to Bogotá. That extra hour seemed to take for ever. We eventually landed, shaken to bits and it was still amazing to see Dad's men get out ahead of us, guns out, ready for anything. As Dad and I remained on the plane, I watched as the bags of cash I'd seen being loaded onto the plane were transferred to the waiting armoured car. I couldn't resist the temptation to take out my trusty old camera and snap a few photos. I had no idea, of course, of the significance of what I was capturing. While we were escorted home, the cash was taken directly to Avenida de Las Américas for safekeeping in the secure vaults.

After my short roll of film was developed, Dad praised me for my photographic achievements. Many of the images from Medellín came out perfectly. He sent the snaps to London where they were included in De La Rue's internal newspaper. I kept a copy of that old publication. It is strangely poignant to look at the images now – a lasting reminder of my last trip to Medellín, the final occasion on which I set eyes on Pablo Escobar, who I still had no idea was my biological father.

CHAPTER 30: THE TRUTH

Madrid, January 1989

'There are things you need to know – for your own safety.'

We were nearing the end of a lovely day spent together when Dad began the conversation that would change my life for ever.

There had seemed nothing unusual when he had asked me to meet him in his penthouse apartment in Calle de Goya, Madrid. I had been looking forward to us hanging out together. We were both living in Spain by then. I was happily married to my lovely wife Sue and was now a father myself, to two beautiful children, and we lived on the Costa del Sol. Life had taken many twists and turns since the family left Colombia. After a turbulent time at Lucton school, I attended art college and was now working as a graphic designer, while harbouring dreams of one day earning my living as an artist. Dad had left De La Rue and was working for the American security company Brink's, based in Madrid, but heading up a taskforce to set up an operation in the United Arab Emirates.

We'd been to the cinema opposite his apartment to see *Full Metal Jacket*, the Vietnam War movie that had just been released in Spain. As Dad reached out to collect our tickets from the box office ticket-seller, I noticed he had something wrong with his hand. It seemed slightly emaciated and he had trouble gripping the tickets. In order to avoid any embarrassment, I had taken the tickets and we went off to buy popcorn and chocolates before the showing. Recently, he hadn't been standing as tall as before, his spine leaning slightly to the left. I'd put this down to the years catching up with him but it troubled me to see this strong, powerful man somehow diminished. When we left the cinema, the air turned chilly but it was a pleasant evening and we decided to walk to a bar further up the road for something to eat. It was there Dad began talking. Clearly there were things he was keen to get off his chest.

'It is time you knew the truth,' he said. He was keen to talk about his life as a policeman in London. It was that role, he said, that had led to him being recruited to the British intelligence service. I sat, stunned, as he explained how he had preferred the night beats as a policeman as it gave him a chance to swat up in the workman's tent on his linguistics courses. A grasp of foreign languages had proved crucial in his new venture working for Arthur Norman.

As Dad spoke, characters from the past flashed into my mind; Sir Arthur, Lady Anne and the office in Regent Street. He explained how he came to be in Colombia, his role with De La Rue and his secret mission and the company's connections with the smuggling gangs. I listened intently, trying to take it all in. Dad, a secret service agent? It was incredible. Yet, oddly, it also made sense. The armed security, the murky connections he had. He mentioned other names, like Clem Chalk. 'Do you remember him?'

'Of course,' I said. 'My favourite memories were his love of all the latest gadgets. When he first showed us a pocket calculator I had no idea what it was. And I remember being jealous of that colour camera that fitted into the palm of his hand.'

'Exactly. Well who do you think it was supplied our clandestine listening devices and recording equipment?'

This was amazing. To think Clem, who often visited with his wife Betty, was in on it too. It was fascinating, almost unbelievable, something you read about happening to other people. We left the bar and walked back to his apartment. Dad had been smiling at his old memories and at my reaction to them but, when we'd settled down to continue our chat, his expression changed.

'There is a reason I am telling you this. It is to do with your real parents. It is for your own safety. There is a very dangerous situation developing.'

I suddenly felt queasy. 'You said there wasn't much known about them.'

Dad bowed his head. 'While that was strictly true, it wasn't the full story.'

'What do you mean?' I asked, nervous about what he might say.

He went to a small bureau and returned with a manila envelope from which he produced a set of old papers. He proceeded to tell me the story of the attack on the armoured truck, the robbery and the mission to recover the stolen money. He didn't spare any detail about the helicopter raid on the village in the hills not far from Bogotá airport. As he was speaking, somehow I knew what was coming. When he got to the part about the fatally injured woman and the baby in the cot the story felt strangely familiar. He showed me the documents, pointing to the relevant information – my mother's name and then, crucially, my name: Roberto Sendoya Escobar.

Roberto? Where had I heard that name before? I couldn't think. It was like something from a dream. 'And my father?' I asked.

'He is named here too.' He pointed to the entry. 'Pablo Escobar'. Although he was a notorious figure worldwide by that point, the name meant nothing to me. 'Do you remember the trips we made to Medellín? The new year parties and the men we met there?' My mind drifted back to those strange events, to the rough-looking men and the one who always took keen notice of me . . . surely not? Dad nodded. 'Don Pablo.'

My mind was in a whirl. This was too much to take in. First, that my mother, my dear, innocent mother, had been killed, in such a terrible way and so young. But now I tried to comprehend that I had met my real father and did not know at the time. Dad could obviously see the confusion and turmoil etched on my face. He explained further about how he had found out about my biological father, how intermediaries had made contact with Escobar and how he had been helping Dad's secret intelligence operation in return for those heavily controlled meetings where he could see me for a very brief moment.

Dad asked again, 'Does the name mean anything to you? Pablo Escobar?' If I was being honest, not much, other than faint memories of hearing these names over the years . . . Escobar . . . Pablo . . . Roberto. Had Escobar called me 'Roberto' once? 'It should,' Dad went on. 'Since those times when we knew him, he has grown to become a very powerful and notorious figure. He became the biggest producer and exporter of cocaine in the world. And he has been responsible for a great many deaths.'

Perhaps the name and the criminal deeds should have meant something to me but I was quite naïve about the world then and didn't even really appreciate what cocaine was. I knew it was a drug but I had no concept of the scale of the operation that Dad talked of. There was no internet to get quickly up to speed on such things. I needed Dad to help me out: 'He has become a very dangerous man, the head of a cocaine smuggling cartel and a ruthless crime boss who thinks nothing of killing anyone who stands in his way. He has built an empire so big it is hard to comprehend. He is also someone who is not satisfied with just being the richest criminal in the world. He craves political power but when that is denied to him – because of his crimes – he exacts bloody vengeance on politicians and judges who thwart his ambitions.'

Dad explained that, over the last few years, Escobar had murdered more than thirty judges. In 1985, when he feared he would be extradited to the US to stand trial for drug crimes, he paid the M-19 guerrilla group a million dollars to launch a terrorist attack on the Colombian palace of justice, take the supreme court hostage and demand an end to the treaty with America. In the siege that followed, nearly a dozen justices alone were killed, along with several terrorists.

'In the last year the violence has got so bad,' Dad went on,' that killings have been reported nearly every day. The government declared martial law because the country is on the brink of descending into all-out war. As Escobar gets more desperate, his grip on power is slipping. His Medellín cartel rivals and his enemies, like the Cali cartel, want to hurt him any way they can, which potentially means targeting his family and, therefore, any children. Someone will know you exist and, if they find out where you are, you could be a target.'

Dad said they had taken precautions to limit the evidence that proved the link between my natural father and me. 'We did our very best to erase these details from your records, son,' he said, 'but I think it's important, now that you are old enough to be able to deal with this, that you should have this old copy. As far as we know, it's the only one in existence and I'm afraid it's all I have. I have been keeping it for when the time was right.'

Dad explained that, as the danger of anyone seeking to settle a score with Escobar was very real, he had arranged for a security team to protect my house. He was true to his word. When I returned to our house in Sotogrande, on the Costa del Sol, I found he had arranged for a former special forces soldier to provide personal protection and uniformed officers to patrol the house. It was like life had gone full circle. After years of living carefree, without the need for security, here I was with protection once more.

Over the next weeks and months Dad and I continued to meet, either in Madrid or at my house, where we would discuss Colombia, my heritage and his secret operations. Sometimes we sat up late, in front of the fire, chatting. Our talks prompted long-buried memories to resurface: I recalled often being asked to walk down, what to me seemed, an unimportant street at the time, while Dad filmed me on his handheld V8 cine-camera, making movies we never saw. I had so many questions. It was hard to process what he was telling me. In some ways it seemed incongruous to think that Dad could be this secret agent, but then there was a delicious irony that this suave, debonair, Savile Row-suited, 6-foot-4-inch-Englishman was, for the majority of his time in Colombia, operating on assignment for the intelligence services in the US and UK. Dad had shown himself to be an expert in the dark arts of the espionage game and his double life was at times mesmerisingly complex. I couldn't help wondering if even his own family was part of his cover story.

We suited both sides of his life. As a businessman in Colombia, where so much stock is placed on family, having children was almost a pre-requisite. Adopting native children – not just me, but Monique too – must have increased his standing considerably among the likes of Gregorio and his friends. Dad was at pains to stress that my godfather knew nothing of the secret operation: his only concern was the success of De La Rue and the respectability the presence of the international firm did for the country. In turn, the work in Colombia had benefited De La Rue itself, as Dad told me: 'The international multi-conglomerate that exists today is the direct result of Operation Durazno.'

He started to tell me some more incredible stories about his activities. He was seeking to unlock for me, the son he clearly loved, the many mysteries of his life in Colombia. He did his best to answer my questions. One thing about my dad – a constant throughout my life – was that, whenever possible, he always told me the truth, no matter how unpleasant it might be.

I wanted to know about my mother. What was she like? What did he think had happened to put her in that house at such a fateful moment? Over time he provided detail that allowed me to piece together the raid on that house. The longer I pondered her cruel fate, the more I was able to make sense of what had haunted my dreams since childhood, the fleeting flashbacks and the excruciatingly loud noises that were indelibly etched in my mind. From hearing Dad's story I assumed the sounds were gunshots which, at the time, I recorded only as an overwhelming, horrific experience. I also had brief visions of a woman in a red dress screaming and a man covered in blood. There was a bottle of baby's milk on the sill of a window that looked out on a street, the interior wall of this room a green colour, paint peeling off. I also recalled a much louder noise alongside the intermittent bangs and, from what my dad told me later, I assumed this came from the helicopters. Those short but deeply disturbing memories had gone unexplained until that conversation with Dad in Madrid, when I probed him for details.

It troubled me deeply to know that I was there in the room when my mother drew her last breath. Yet I could take comfort from the fact that it was my adopted dad – the one I had always looked on as my real and only father – who ensured the gunfight that day did not claim one more victim – me. Dad confirmed that he believed her pregnancy would not have been planned – and, until the fact of my existence was made known to Escobar, he probably didn't give me much thought, if he even knew I had been born at all. I found that also disturbing to think about. What a short, tragic life my mother led. The more I learned about my real father the more I realised what a despicable character he must be.

But what intrigued me was finding out how much I was like him. And how much did he benefit from the attention heaped on him by Operation Durazno? As Dad said, early on in our discussions: 'The rise of the cartels didn't happen by accident.'

No one could have predicted back then how big Escobar would become but there was an element of design as well as luck to his success. It suited the American and British intelligence service to have just the one kingpin in the drug business, someone they could monitor and, to a degree, control. What they didn't account for was how firmly he would grasp the opportunity presented to him. By ruthlessly murdering rivals and coming up with ingenious methods of smuggling cocaine into the US, he made more money than anyone could believe.

In 1975 he was already shipping hundreds of kilograms into the US at a time. Millions of dollars quickly turned into billions. Even when he was arrested, he was able to buy his way out of trouble. He believed that money and power could get him anything he wanted – almost anything.

For Dad, the kidnap attempt at the Calatrava and the subsequent attack on the armoured car that killed Barandiga showed Escobar was getting out of control. He couldn't ensure our safety any more so he moved us out of Colombia. Through the sale of our home he rented two properties in Santo Domingo – the penthouse apartment and the beachfront property he had promised me.

Speaking to Dad about this period of my life awakened memories I'd long since buried about my school life as much as about Colombia. I recalled when I arrived at Lucton I realised my feelings of foreboding hadn't been unfounded. There never seemed to be enough food and we shuffled around permanently hungry. House masters dished out canings for any misdemeanour and, for a while, it was a miserable existence. I missed my family greatly and felt very homesick. I grew resilient, however, formed alliances, threw myself into the sports I loved like rugby and fencing and somehow managed to make the most of it.

In the summer I flew to the Dominican Republic and, as Dad had predicted, found a very different life there to the one we had in Colombia. He had hired me a new bodyguard, called Lorenzo, and I enjoyed the luxury of a chauffeur-driven car to use when hanging out with my friends. Although my security was always prominent, I began to have more freedom.

At first, as Dad had said would happen, whenever possible I joined him on his business trips in the little Cessna plane. As the years progressed, though, I saw less of him. He headed up the launch of De La Rue's operations in the country but he was still flying to Colombia to work on the ongoing Operation Durazno.

By 1977, however, Escobar was becoming more elusive. He became a father once again when his wife gave birth to their first child together, a son called Juan. Two years later Escobar constructed the opulent mansion of which he had always dreamed. Hacienda Los Nápoles was a 7,400-acre ranch and country estate by the Magdalena River, eighty miles from Medellín. It cost him $75 million and he built swimming pools, several lakes, a network of roads and an airport and flew in dozens of exotic animals such as rhinos, hippos and camels, to create his own personal zoo.

Already his cartel controlled more than half of the cocaine flooding the US. To those who encountered him in those early days he had a guile that elevated him above the usual criminal. He was ruthless and vicious, undoubtedly, but he had an interest in politics and an eye for public relations almost unrivalled in the underworld. As he grew wealthier he bankrolled the campaigns of those politicians who would look after his interests.

In 1978 he decided to enter politics himself. He stood as a substitute council member for Medellín (in Colombia, voters elect both an official and a substitute). He was duly elected, which wasn't hard when he could easily outspend all of his rivals put together. His money also influenced the presidential elections that year, helping to propel his chosen candidate, Julio Turbay, to power. Three years later, he stood for congress, again as a substitute, and was elected; a clever move as, once he entered congress, he was immune from prosecution.

In no time he owned more than a dozen properties, a fleet of boats, his own planes and even a couple of submarines to aid his cocaine smuggling operation. Aside from his own ridiculous personal wealth, he used his position in congress to fund social housing, leisure and business projects in his native Medellín, fuelling the myth that he was some sort of Robin Hood figure. He didn't just want to be successful and rich, he wanted to be revered. His ambition was to rid his native city of slums. His cartel had turned cocaine production into the biggest industry in Colombia. From the money flooding into the economy he boosted construction and created thousands of jobs for the unemployed.

Dad's work in Medellín had ceased by then but up until 1978 he had been tracking the cartel's money and helping Escobar to siphon off a personal stash himself, unknown to his smuggling partners. Escobar seemed to be untouchable, revelling in a climate in which drug smuggling was practically tolerated in both Colombia and the US. In the States, cocaine was largely viewed as a party drug, used by professionals as a way to let off steam. In Colombia, because of the boost to the economy, many people were ambivalent about the smugglers, believing them to be pioneers in the same way liquor and tobacco racketeers had been. While the money was rolling in and everyone seemed to be benefitting it appeared as though Pablo Escobar and his cartel could do no wrong.

Then the tide began to turn. Politicians in the USA began to sit up and take notice of such vast sums of dollars leaking from the country and threatening to do harm to the most powerful economy on the planet. By the end of the decade, the picture had become murkier. JB spent more time in Panama, running multiple intelligence operations. His relationship with the US became perilous when they suspected him of sharing information with communist Cuba. When the Panamanian dictator and ally of JB, Omar Torrijos, was killed in a plane crash in 1981 it set in motion a chain of events that saw Noriega become leader of the country, some two years later. He had the power he had long craved but it began to look as if his closeness to the drug cartels could be his undoing. That JB was in reality Manuel Noriega was another stunning revelation for me.

Noriega's rise through the ranks of the Panamanian security services had given him a unique position from which to run his operations. On one hand he had his legitimate job as an intelligence officer, which would often bring him in to contact with the CIA and, on the other, he had his own ambitions to take over the presidency one day, no doubt a significantly costly affair that necessitated his dealings with the young but flourishing cartels of Colombia.

The many deals Noriega cut with the gangs while acting as a CIA informant on drugs en route to the US were bound to come back and bite him one day. Playing the ruthless cartel and the US government off each other was a perilous business. Yet, in the early years, the cash coming back from the US had nowhere to go other than straight back to the Colombian cartels, and in well over eighty per cent of the cases, to the Medellín cartel.

Escobar's golden touch deserted him when he tried to take his seat in congress in 1983. On this occasion he was publicly denounced as a drug trafficker with previous convictions and he was humiliated, his dreams of one day becoming president in tatters. Although became a father for the third time in 1984 with the birth of Manuela, his vengeance on those responsible for his political downfall began the same year with the murder, on his orders, of Rodrigo Lara, the politician who had denounced him in congress. That sparked a powerful response from congress.

He was stripped of his seat and, in the midst of a heavy crackdown on his operation he fled to Panama, where Noriega, his old Durazno connection, gave him safe haven.

By 1989, with Noriega only just clinging to power, having fallen foul of the US administration under George Bush, Escobar was also losing his grip on his own empire. As someone who believed he had single-handedly clawed his way up from the slums – conveniently forgetting who had helped him along the way – he was not going to go down without a fight. Living on the run back in Colombia, the net closing in around him as his political enemies tried to have him extradited to the US to face justice and his cartel rivals vowing to muscle in on his territory, he retaliated the only way he knew how – by exacting more bloody revenge.

It was almost as though Dad knew the right time had come to share his secrets. Only a few months after he began his revelations, a number of events thrust my natural father into the international spotlight: Escobar's notoriety grew when *Forbes* magazine listed him as the seventh-richest man in the world; the frontrunner in the forthcoming Colombian presidential election, Luis Carlos Galán, an outspoken critic of Escobar's, was shot dead at a campaign rally; three months later, Galán's political stand-in, César Gaviria, another who condemned Escobar, only just cheated death. Gaviria was to fly on Avianca Flight 203 from Bogotá to Cali. On the advice of his security team he changed his plans at the last minute. The plane exploded five minutes after take-off, killing all 107 people on board as well as three on the ground. It was the deadliest single criminal attack during all the decades of violence in Colombia.

Against this backdrop I should have been even more fearful for my life. I had much bigger things to worry about than my own health, however. One day – and without warning – something happened that destroyed my life completely.

CHAPTER 31: THE LAST SECRET REVEALED

I first noticed something was wrong when Sue started walking around in circles at home, complaining of a piercing headache. At first, I thought maybe she had had one drink too many but that thought was quickly dispelled. From the look on her face I could tell something was seriously wrong.

I took her to a private doctor in Marbella. He was one of the first in the Costa del Sol to offer a CT scan, the computerised brain imaging diagnosis tool, and he saw her straight away. Once he had the results he told me to come quickly. She didn't come into the consulting room herself but the doctor showed me an image of a growth the size of a tennis ball in her skull. The doctor said that without an operation in the next few days she would die. Sue was waiting outside to hear the outcome. It was down to me to break it to her. 'I am so sorry,' I said, trying to keep a lid on my emotions. 'You have a brain tumour. The doctor says you need an operation immediately.'

She was understandably shocked, but there was no time to feel sorry for ourselves. We had to get help, fast. The doctor had recommended a specialist in Gibraltar. I took Sue immediately but it was no use. To our horror and great sorrow, he said her condition was too advanced and he couldn't help. Our only option was to get back to London as soon as possible, where we could seek help at the Charing Cross hospital. It felt as though our lives were falling to pieces around us. I was in a terrible panic at that point, but I tried to think rationally. I called Sue's parents, John and Mary, to come and look after our children while we flew to London. At the Charing Cross the doctor carried out another scan but it was the same outcome. 'There's nothing I can do,' he said. 'It is a stage three myeloma.' He explained that stage three meant the tumour was terminal. 'Your wife will be dead in a couple of weeks.'

I couldn't believe it. We were devastated. As I held her in my arms, our short life together flashed before my eyes: we'd met not long after I graduated from the City & Guilds of London Art School. I was working in a hotel and had moved into a flat in Walton-on-Thames, Surrey. Just along the Thames was the Chertsey Lock nightclub and that's where I saw her for the first time – and fell in love completely. Her name was Sue Hobbs, she was nine years older than me and was working as a window dresser. I was struck by Cupid's arrow and before long I moved in with her at her place in Stoke Poges, near Slough. I planned to ask her to marry me back at the place where we first met and we had a night at Chertsey Lock, where I had booked a table.

At the right moment, I produced the ring, popped the question and . . . she burst out laughing and pointed at my head. I was confused. I was no expert but I was sure this wasn't the usual reaction. I swiftly realised that, in my nervous excitement, I'd leant too close to a candle and my hair was now on fire. She called a waiter who sprang to my aid, unceremoniously dousing my head with his soda fountain.

Less than a year after our first meeting, we were having our wedding. I wrote to Gregorio, inviting him to come. Sadly, however, by then he was suffering from Parkinson's disease and was unable to travel. It would have been lovely to be reacquainted with my beloved godfather. He replied with a telegram wishing us all the best for the future. It was the last time I ever heard from him.

For Sue and me, life improved immeasurably with the arrival of our first child, Jonathan, in 1985. We gave him the middle name John to honour Sue's father. When our daughter was born in 1988 our family was complete. We called her Anna – with the middle name May, in memory of my dear grandmother at whose home I had spent such long and wonderful summers. By then we were living in Spain, where we'd moved when I got the opportunity to take a job as a graphic designer. Sue was incredibly supportive, viewing the change as a big adventure. She wasn't just my wife; she was my partner and best friend. I couldn't bear the thought of losing her. It didn't seem fair. Our lives should have been just beginning together, not on the verge of being torn apart.

In the aftermath of that terrible prognosis, we were faced with a decision. We did not know how long we had left but I was determined that she had access to the best care available. I moved her in with my parents at Gainsborough Court, Walton-on-Thames, the house that Dad bought with the proceeds of selling the Calatrava estate house in Colombia, while I returned to Spain to look after the children and work out a short-term solution.

Sue went on a programme of radiotherapy and, for three months, Dad took her for her treatment. She maintained a positive attitude for as long as she could and defied the doctor's bleak prediction, surviving for three years. Eventually, however, it was a fight too big even for her. She tragically passed away in 1993. I was by her side when she died, wishing until the end for some miracle to spare her. Just one month later I would be doing the same thing again for another person I loved dearly, devastated that a second incredible story was coming to an end.

*

On one of those memorable evenings in Madrid, in that period when Dad opened up about his life, he asked me to accompany him for a short walk. As he said this, he pointed to his left ear with an exaggerated gesture and waved his hands towards various parts of the ceiling. I got it straight away. He thought his flat might be bugged. Given what he had already disclosed within these walls I could hardly even imagine what was coming next.

A few minutes' walk led us to the corner of a fairly ordinary street lined on both sides by high-rise apartment blocks. The only activity was that of a couple of maids, hanging out washing on the balconies, and the only sound was a distant radio. Most of the other balcony balustrades were draped in pot plants that spilled over and hung down to make a kind of static green waterfall. Dad stopped at a gate leading into a basement parking facility belonging to a relatively modern block. It was sandwiched between much higher, older buildings. Dad signalled for me to look at the small set of buttons situated on an aluminium panel at about eye-level on the left of the garage door. There was another panel just above these buttons with what looked like a card-swipe facility.

'Only someone with the right card can enter,' he said.

As he swiped, the vast garage door burst into life and opened upwards. From the depths of the cavernous interior, I could see the faint glimmer of a lift door. Dad explained there was a special storage area further down, accessible through another card-operated lock. I assumed we would be using the lift but Dad shook his head and closed the outer door again. 'It is here we hide the cash,' he whispered.

On the way back to the apartment I asked what he meant. To my complete and utter amazement he proceeded to tell me. When Escobar was in fear of being extradited and effectively living on the run, unable to return to his luxury estate and constantly moving to avoid capture, he started to make contingency plans. At the height of his operation,

Escobar was making so much money he could not spend it all. Some of it was stashed into the walls of houses, some was buried, some he lost track of. Yet some of the cash, while not immediately accessible to him, he did control – a large amount he'd siphoned off for Dad to hide for him way back in 1976. This was secretly moved from De La Rue's vaults to the underground store in Madrid. Dad did not expand on how they did it, but I suspected they'd used a private charter flight. I remembered that rattling old DC-4 they chartered to move Escobar's cash from Medellín to Bogotá around the same time.

We were almost back at the apartment when I asked Dad if we could go down in the lift to see what was in the basement. He pondered the request for a moment. 'OK. Tomorrow.' I had trouble sleeping that night, imagining what would be revealed in that underground vault. It would be the start of another adventure.

We had a quick breakfast in a nearby café where the waiter knew Dad so well that he didn't even have to make an order. When we arrived at the garage I imagined the big metal door was all that stood between me and piles of neatly stacked dollars. Dad swiped his card and the door juddered and grinded open. We entered the gloomy interior that smelled of damp cement and diesel. All I could make out in the semi-darkness were a few boxes and some rusty old portable generators partially covered by a tarpaulin sheet. Dad produced a little pocket torch and, with its beam lighting the way, we crept towards the back and the small elevator door. A swipe of a second card brought the lift to life. Inside, there weren't many buttons, Dad pressed the bottom one and we descended. He shone the torch ahead as we ventured out. Just as I was thinking we were going to have to feel our way in the dark, Dad found the light switch. The flickering tubes instantly transformed the room. I was taken aback, not only by the sudden light, but also by the sight of a pile of black sacks neatly placed on a pallet in the middle of the room. It was not quite the mountain of dollars I imagined but it was intriguing nonetheless.

I approached the sacks and looked to Dad for approval. He gestured for me to go ahead. There were four sacks, each about the size of a large sports bag. I looked for an opening in the top one. I had to jostle it to get it into position and was surprised at how heavy it was. More memories of Dad's people carrying the bags from Medellín off the DC-4 all those years ago came flooding back. Could this be one of those sacks? This was now a much more exciting prospect and, as I pulled the sack open, I caught sight of neatly wrapped bundles of notes. They were American dollars bundled in tight cellophane wrapping. A thin strip denoting the denomination value enveloped the bundles, which were about an inch thick. Those I could read were hundred-dollar bundles. If they were the same all the way through, there was a considerable amount of money here. Dad's tap on the shoulder and hand gesture directed my attention to another part of the room. To the right, about ten feet away, a sheet of tarpaulin was draped over another large shape, several feet high. We lifted the canvas sheet together to reveal around six or seven more of these black sacks. Having put everything back as we had found it, we made our way to the lift. I wanted to talk about it all, but it didn't seem like the right time. For some reason I couldn't express, silence was the appropriate response to seeing all that money.

On the route home to Dad's apartment we walked through a park and I mustered up the courage to ask him about the money. He told me De La Rue had started to collect money from criminal gangs way back in 1965. The money came from a variety of sources for some years but, latterly, it was all from Escobar and, due to the special relationship with Dad, included Pablo's own personal stash. Some of it had been used to build the Calatrava estate and what I'd seen represented a portion of that which he had been able to get out of the country. Dad believed it amounted to several hundred million dollars but he said it was virtually impossible to use in any straightforward way. It had been brought out of Colombia once the authorities there had started to tighten the noose on the Medellín cartel. Most of the cash had already been moved from Madrid. This was all that was left of a much larger horde.

Dad and I never mentioned the money again and he never said what happened to those last remaining sacks in Madrid. Other things took precedence. To begin with, my wife's illness was my main concern but, as we nursed her over the few remaining years of her life, we realised we had to face another terrible truth. Dad's own health was deteriorating rapidly. From the curvature of his spine to his weakened hand, we saw a rapid decline in his movement and stature.

His physical condition had really started to get bad when he worked in Pakistan in the late 1980s. He was in Karachi when he caught diphtheria, a highly contagious and potentially life-threatening infection of the nose and throat. On his return he was kept in the Hospital For Tropical Diseases in London. He was kept in over Christmas and we had to don full medical gear to see him because of the risk of infection. He eventually recovered, but the toxins must have had a lasting effect. When he heeded our repeated pleas to see a specialist, he was diagnosed with motor neurone disease. Tragically, over the same period that Sue was receiving radiotherapy to prolong her life, Dad went downhill fast. Eventually, I had to answer the phone for him as he was too weak to speak. My mother struggled to cope so I tried to do as much for him as I could.

It broke my heart to see this powerful chap so diminished. I loved him to bits and admired him for fighting evil on behalf of the government. His operation in Karachi had been successful. By 1991 a long-running investigation into the Bank of Credit and Commerce International (BCCI), which once had been the seventh-largest bank in the world, resulted in its offices in several countries being raided and its records seized. Among many crimes being investigated were money-laundering practices on behalf of a number of notorious figures and organisations, including, curiously enough, the Medellín cartel and Manuel Noriega. So wide did the corruption extend that investigators began referring to BCCI as the 'Bank of Crooks and Criminals International' for the amount of business done with regimes and organisations that dealt in arms and drugs. The bank was shut down and its directors indicted.

I owed everything to my father. He saved my life many times over. Without him, who knows if I would have made it out of that remote Colombian house alive? He had given me a home and an education and, even when that looked like it wasn't paying off, he provided the means for me to ultimately follow my dreams. I remembered being sixteen, on the balcony of our house in Santo Domingo, Dad sitting in the rocking chair that would follow him back to England. He said: 'Your education has cost a lot of money. What have you learned from it all?'

'Dad,' I said, 'I might not have done all that great in my exams but I have learned one thing.'

'And what's that?'

'I've learned that you do what you can to get around the rules without getting caught.'

He laughed. 'You're such a Colombiano.'

'Don't worry, Dad,' I said, 'by the time I am twenty-two I will be a millionaire.'

I had no idea how significant those words were; not because I came close to achieving that bold ambition but because, years later, I would discover that it was the same pronouncement my natural father made at a similar age. When I spoke like that, I think Dad understood that I was a bit of a rebel. He could see that side of my nature and, knowing the stock I had come from, he was perhaps concerned about the direction I might take upon leaving school.

On some level he had a right to be concerned. He didn't know the half of what I got up to at school, apart from the misdemeanours that resulted in letters home. Perhaps due to my fiery temper, I got into a lot of fights. I was also party to several moments of highjinks, like the time when the headmaster's car ended up on the tennis courts. Such boisterousness I would take years to work out of my system, perhaps not until I left school and played rugby, latterly for Weybridge Vandals, and fencing, which I really took to and at which I went on to represent the all-England club in my capacity as second sabre. When I was still at school, I struggled academically but, as I told Dad, I developed the wits needed to survive a place like Lucton.

I had always loved drawing and painting and it was Dad, while I was at boarding school, who encouraged this passion. He arranged for me to have a tutor – and what a teacher it was. Roy Reynolds, a descendant of Sir Joshua Reynolds, the founding president of the Royal Academy of Arts in London, was a realist painter who taught me the many tricks of painting. I used to cycle from the school for our private lessons. He showed me how to use layers of paint sitting inside varnishes to achieve vibrancy, which I used to achieve translucent effects in my own work. At the City & Guilds of London Art School I studied under its principal, Roger de Grey. That learning gave me a foundation to later develop a technique of my own and forge a career as an artist. Sadly, Dad would not survive long enough to see me fully benefit from the education he helped provide.

Dad's condition deteriorated until we had no choice but to admit him to Walton-on-Thames Cottage hospital in 1993. As I had done for Sue, I often sat on his bedside holding his terribly emaciated hand. On one occasion two nurses approached the bedside and asked Dad if he wanted a drink of water. By this stage of his illness he was sipping little gulps through a straw that had to be held for him. It was so sad to see a man who had done such great things reduced to this pitiful wreck. I felt utterly powerless and, as he gazed into my eyes, I could feel his emotional pain. His shallow breathing was accompanied by a rattling sound that I knew signalled the end was near. I will always remember the haunting, glazed stare of his eyes.

Once the nurses had gone, he became agitated. His voice, which was practically incoherent by now, seemed to reach me. Any movement he made required enormous amounts of effort. I was therefore hypersensitive to anything he was trying to say. It was almost as if nothing else mattered. The world outside the little hospital became irrelevant. My whole life was, for this fleeting moment, concentrated on the dreadful tragedy being played out in front of me. The stuttering sounds and the tiny gestures were all I needed. We understood each other perfectly.

Somehow, I knew he wanted something from his faithful old DAKS jacket. Throughout his life he had carried a slim-line diary in the top inside pocket. The contact details of anyone who was anyone in his world of secrets had been jotted down on the pages of this treasure, albeit with no clue included as to their importance. I handed it to him. Tragically, his grasp was failing and it fell open on the bed. In doing so, a piece of paper slipped out on to the blanket. On one side it had the letterhead of the Home Office nationality department in Tolworth, Surrey. The neatly typed letter, dated 23 August 1967, confirmed my British nationality had been accepted. As I read it, Dad signalled with a finger to turn over. On the back were some strange symbols and some numbers.

M 25 . . . . TWO / 5s. = 10.°

M 14 . . . . TWO / 4s.6d = 9.°

Dad beckoned me close. I could just make out his whispered words. 'The cash . . . remember.' It was so hard to understand him now. Another gargantuan effort brought forward the same words, only this time he added, 'Madrid.'

I looked again at the symbols and numbers. It looked like some kind of addition or quick sum one would write in a rush on the back of an envelope. I asked, 'Is this where the money is?'

His brief smile and relaxed shoulders were all I needed as confirmation. His feeble body sunk back into the soft pillows. I could see he was ready. I couldn't bear it; it was so painful. I was going to be alone, with no one to look up to any more. The nurses arrived and suggested I let him rest. They assured me that when his breathing slowed down they would call me. It wasn't long before they did.

My beloved dad's life ended with dignity and strength that day. For him, a remarkable story was finally over.

For me, it was just beginning.

EPILOGUE

Another story came to an end in 1993.

Just months after my wife and then my dad passed away, justice finally caught up with my real father. While my adopted father was bravely battling a terminal condition, my real father was cowardly trying to escape his own destiny. With his options rapidly running out and a bloody campaign that ended in the deaths of multiple kidnap victims, including that of Diana Turbay, the journalist daughter of one of his earliest political allies, the former president Julio Turbay, Escobar gave himself up.

Still desperately trying to evade extradition to the US, he hatched a deal with Colombia's president, César Gaviria, that he would serve a sentence in a prison of his choosing, as long as a law was passed prohibiting extradition. Driven by the desire to end the violence ripping Colombia apart, Gaviria agreed and the law was passed. Escobar, however, made a mockery of the deal, building his own lavish prison, La Catedral, and turning it into a luxury holiday home for him and his *sicarios*. He continued to run the cartel but, in July 1992, when the government learned murders had been committed inside the prison, they attempted to move the drug baron to a more secure unit. Escobar fled and spent the next sixteen months of the run, living in a series of boltholes, his vast wealth suddenly useless and his empire crumbling.

Eventually, on 2 December 1993, Search Bloc, a crack police unit, tracked Escobar to his hideout in the middle-class barrio of Los Olivos, Medellín. As the armed unit closed in, Escobar and a bodyguard tried to flee across rooftops, but he was shot in the leg and body. A fatal shot through the ear finished him off. The 'king of cocaine' was dead. In an attempt to perpetuate the myth that the fearless outlaw evaded justice to the end, some of his relatives claimed he killed himself when cornered, rather than face arrest. To many in his native city he died a hero, with 25,000 citizens turning out for his funeral.

I found out about my biological father's death watching the evening news. My initial reaction was a feeling of huge relief. It was over. He was dead, although it was far from an end for the drug trade. Following the death or arrest of other leading players in his organisation, the Cali cartel became the dominant force, picking up where their rivals in Medellín had left off.

For me, relief soon gave way to a very real fear. For the last three or four years, since Dad's revelations, I'd been struggling to process what he was telling me. I'd had the double trauma of losing two people I loved. Now, with my natural father dead, I began to worry. Would there be reprisals? While he had been alive had I benefitted from a weird safety net, a level of protection that his exalted status provided? And, now that he was gone, would the rivals who had hated him so much be out for revenge? Whichever way I looked at it, I was an unwitting heir to an empire of unimaginable wealth, power and violence. The fact that I was born illegitimate and had since been adopted was surely irrelevant: I was still the eldest son of Pablo Escobar. That could make me an asset to some and a threat to others.

I remembered all the guards we had at the house, the twenty-four-hour security. I suffered flashbacks from the time people broke into the house or tried to snatch me on the street. Had Escobar wanted to kidnap me or murder me? I like to think he wanted me back, but there was no way of knowing.

I thought back to those strange meetings I had with him. Whenever I saw him in Medellín, he wore the same type of clothing: casual, open-necked shirt and not especially smart trousers held up by a belt. His hair was often untidy and greasy. The fleeting memories of this man had stuck in my mind and I always had the sense there was something unusual about our get-togethers, but it wasn't until Dad told me the stories in Madrid that I grew to understand the reasons for these half-hour contact sessions with my real father. This grand annual event was the occasion on which allegiances were confirmed. Monique was never present; she was with Otilia in our hotel bedroom.

As I grew older – and once I knew I was adopted – life became a little more complicated because I now knew I had another father out there. I felt a strange sense of guilt, perhaps a feeling of disloyalty, for even thinking about asking questions. My adoptive parents didn't disclose to me that I had been meeting my genetic father once a year, nor had I been told that the other man I would meet regularly was one of Escobar's people, entrusted with keeping an eye on me. Silvio, who I met at the *finca* with Dad, would pop up on quite a regular basis during my Colombian childhood. Later, he even came to visit me at my prep school in England.

The end result of all of this was that I spent the majority of my childhood not knowing the truth about my heritage. At boarding school in England, I never disclosed the fact that I was adopted, nor did I share with anyone the details of my life that I did know. I felt a kind of shame because I desperately wanted Dad to be my real father. Once I knew I was adopted, I felt a conflict in my mind that has, in many respects, affected my whole life.

Whether Escobar wanted me back or whether he wanted me kept at a safe distance has never been made clear to me. What is certain is that, because of his rise to prominence, I was vulnerable to being kidnapped, and my adopted father was obviously well-aware of this, particularly after the early kidnap attempt, which is why I had my own bodyguards.

I have often wondered why I only met my real father once a year and why we stopped going to Medellín after some years. Perhaps it was because of the escalating, narcotics-fuelled violence in Colombia or, more likely, because in 1976 Escobar's interest may have been diverted by his marriage to Maria Victoria Henao. Whatever the reason, after that last meeting and the glimpse at the airport in 1976, I never saw the man from Medellín again.

After Escobar's death I found everything almost too much to take. I continued with the close protection and had a sophisticated alarm system fitted on my house. For a long time I lived in fear of my life and those of my children. Gradually, however, things settled down and I felt able to live a normal life again – whatever normal was. In an attempt to process all that had happened, I began researching what Dad had told me. I tried to find out what records existed for my biological mother. Sadly, there were none. It seemed Dad was telling the truth when he said he handed me all the evidence there was that I actually existed.

I looked into the history of De La Rue. I discovered references to Sir Arthur's colourful past. Intriguingly, one newspaper report said De La Rue's personnel were used to 'danger and secrecy'. It went on to say that the company 'has routinely employed former military specialists, many of them linguists with an intelligence background, and has close ties with the Foreign Office and the Secret Intelligence Service, MI6'. I almost could not believe it when it also said that 'in the world in which they operate, murders, coups, espionage and dirty tricks are routine'. It was an astonishingly accurate appraisal of Operation Durazno.

As I continued my research, I was intrigued by the names on my adoption certificate. Gregorio, of course, had played a large and significant role in my life. He was not only my godfather but also the principal witness of my adoption at the notary. As Dad said, Gregorio was kept in the dark about De La Rue's clandestine operations, but he knew all about my adoption and helped make it happen. It was the less familiar names on that document that now held my attention. Some were people I knew from my childhood. Back then, I knew them as paternal uncles, nice guys who visited the house regularly. Uncle Carlos Echeverri, my legal representative in my adoption, was also the representative of a young lady called Anita Uribe, the girl who officially put me up for adoption. I discovered her family were very well-connected politically and, being a minor herself, she would conveniently be required to have a legal representative present at the notary.

I didn't think this was particularly significant, until I looked into the family name Uribe. Álvaro Uribe was president of Colombia from 2002 to 2010 and was born in 1952 in Medellín. In a document generated by the United States Defence Intelligence Agency in 1991, Uribe appeared on a list of the names of the most important drug dealers in Colombia. He was described as a collaborator of the Medellín cartel and a friend of Pablo Escobar and was also accused of possessing financial interests in companies engaged in drug trafficking and, it was said, he had assisted the cartel with regard to extradition laws.

Uribe has always strenuously denied these claims and the allegations were not backed up by hard evidence. Indeed, when he was in office he became a staunch enemy of narcotics traffickers and his administration was responsible for arresting and extraditing more drug traffickers to the United States than all other presidents to date. I found it interesting, though, that a connection existed through the family name, from my adopted parents to my natural father.

Another link between my adoptive family and Pablo Escobar was Manuel Noriega. The USA had maintained numerous military bases and a substantial garrison to protect the American-owned Panama Canal and to maintain US control of this strategically important area. On 7 September 1977, US president Jimmy Carter and the de facto leader of Panama, General Omar Torrijos, signed the Torrijos–Carter Treaties, which set in motion the process of handing over the canal to Panama control by 2000. The US military bases remained, and one condition of the transfer was that the canal would remain open for American shipping.

The US had long-standing relations with Noriega, who served as an intelligence asset and paid informant of the CIA from 1967, including the period in which future president George Bush was head of the agency from 1976-1977. Noriega had sided with the US rather than the USSR in Central America, notably in sabotaging the forces of the Sandinista government in Nicaragua, and the revolutionaries of the FMLN group in El Salvador. Noriega received upwards of $100,000 per year from the 1960s until the 1980s, when his salary was increased to $200,000. Although he worked with the American drug enforcement authority to restrict illegal drug shipments, he was known to simultaneously accept significant financial support from drug dealers, facilitating the laundering of drug money. The gangs also received protection from DEA (Drug Enforcement Agency) investigations, due to Noriega's special relationship with the CIA.

Dad often saw Noriega in Panama but if they were meeting in Colombia, it would almost always be at the Club Campestre, Ibagué. Dad never actually named his Panamanian connection to me, but it was obvious that Noriega had to be the principal he was working with. He was the only Panamanian CIA operative with a direct line to the Medellín cartel at the time.

In January 1975, I was with Dad on the golf course at the club when he met his connection. I had my own little camera with me, as I usually did, and happily snapped away, as I always did on family outings. I took this particular image quickly as I knew photos of his business meetings were not something Dad approved of. His world of secrets merged seamlessly with our family life, which is why I often met those whom he was working with, without really knowing who they were. It was only years later when, armed with Dad's revelations, I started to piece together nuggets of his details with my own memories. At last I understood why he was always traveling to Panama and Nicaragua throughout my childhood.

The cocaine smugglers had their own methods of laundering their cash, but they had their limits. Over five years or so, with the help of Noriega's connections, Operation Durazno was able to infiltrate the cartels to an extent that De La Rue was trusted to expand the criminals' cash transportation abilities for them. Even these powerful drug gangs had their enemies and shipments of cash often went missing (with dire consequences for those entrusted with its safe delivery). But it was one thing knowing who was involved in moving such vast quantities of drugs and quite another getting hard proof. My dad and his various connections were able to add significantly to the undercover work being undertaken by several other agencies in Colombia. Ultimately, this would help unmask the main operatives and chief beneficiaries of the drug trade.

As is recorded in the annals of history, Noriega was, to all intents and purposes, playing his own game by lining his pockets with payoffs from both sides. Eventually, he was able to become ruler of his own country. Like Escobar, who he grew so close to in the course of his work, he became corrupted by power. There were echoes of the 1970 situation in Colombia when, during the Panamanian national elections in May 1989, Noriega refused to accept the result when an alliance of parties opposed to his dictatorship counted results from the country's election precincts before they were sent to the district centres. According to their tallies, Guillermo Endara, their preferred candidate, had defeated

Carlos Duque, the choice of the pro-Noriega coalition by nearly 3–1. As things turned nasty, Noriega supporters assaulted Endara as he attempted a victory motorcade.

Noriega declared the election null and desperately tried to cling on to power by force, a move that proved deeply unpopular with his own people. Despite protests, Noriega's government insisted it had won the presidential election and blamed US-backed candidates in the opposition parties for causing irregularities in the results. As international tensions mounted, President Bush called on Noriega to honour the decision of the Panamanian electorate and relinquish his grip on power. The US put more pressure on Noriega's regime by stepping up its military presence at the canal.

Noriega also faced a coup from his own armed forces but in October foiled an attempt to unseat him by members of the Panamanian defence forces. As the future of the nation hung in the balance, President Bush branded Noriega a drug trafficker and refused to negotiate with him. He denied having any knowledge of Noriega's involvement with the drug trade, even though Bush had met with Noriega while he was director of the CIA and had been the chair of the task force on drugs while he served as vice president to Ronald Reagan.

On 15 December, the Panamanian general assembly declared a state of war with the USA, which responded by mounting an invasion. The USA said that, as well as safeguarding the lives of American citizens, defending democracy and protecting the integrity of the Torrijos–Carter Treaties, it was combating drug trafficking. It branded Panama, under Noriega, a centre for drug money laundering and a transit point for trafficking to the US and Europe. The invasion lasted just over a month and ended with Noriega's capture and imprisonment in the US for seventeen years.

The sweet irony of it all, however, was that the operation Noriega had helped to set up ultimately led the USA to his door as cartel banker. He was far from the only one to be ultimately ruined partly because of an association with my natural father.

Escobar's legacy is one of devastation and destruction. He ruined countless lives, either through the drugs he mercilessly flooded the world with, or through his mindless violence. It is a terrible burden to bear, knowing your natural father was a mass murderer who peddled misery, growing obscenely wealthy as a result. For a long time, I wasn't sure I could cope. I worried how much of his impulsive personality I had inherited and whether I should atone for his actions.

When I pieced the events of my life together with the established facts of history I began to realise that the most effective way to process it all was to write it down. My motivation was not only to get the truth out but, in some small way, to alleviate some of the suffering his crimes caused by giving back to the communities most harmed by the scourge of drugs. And, so, fifteen years ago I began writing, first on an old typewriter that used to belong to my Uncle Jack. The more I researched the more incredible the story became. If I hadn't had my own memories – and the photos I took at the time, which cemented the recollections in my mind – I would have thought it was too unlikely to be true.

Over the course of my research, I even learned that Pablo Escobar had a connection to Queen Elizabeth through his adopted family. My dear old grandmother May was related to John Aird, an extra equerry to the Queen. His father, Sir John Aird, first baronet, was the civil engineer whose firm built the first Aswan Dam across the Nile and was involved in dismantling and moving the iconic Crystal Palace buildings from the 1851 Great Exhibition in Hyde Park to Sydenham in the south-east of London. In a further genealogical twist, my adopted mother Joan's sister married Colin Owen, the brother of the celebrated First World War poet Wilfred

Owen. It was quite a family on my mother's side. If only the 'king of cocaine' knew how close he came to real royalty. Perhaps he would have stepped up his attempts to kidnap his first born son.

After Dad's death, Joan continued to live in Walton-on-Thames until she passed away in 2014. Sadly, my adopted sister Monique had died from a stroke three years earlier. That leaves me as the last one standing from our little family unit in Colombia. In recent years I found love again, with Julie Murphy, a nurse who I met, as many people do these days, online. She has been wonderful for me. Her calm, down-to-earth manner is the perfect foil for my occasional excitability. I owe her a debt of gratitude as without her love and support I would not have been able to write this book and deal with the emotional turmoil it stirred up. After the heartache of losing my first wife, Julie taught me how to laugh and love again. Six years ago we moved to Majorca where I became an artist, painting landscapes using the techniques I learned from my illustrious tutors all those years ago.

Revisiting my childhood in Colombia, like returning to Spain, has shown me that, in life, many things turn full circle. Despite my own challenging time at Lucton, I have found myself involved in the school. Since my days there, Lucton has enjoyed a transformation and is now one of the top establishments of its kind in the country. It is an honour to be associated with it once again after all those years.

Some other things are equally hard to let go. At my house I still have the old rocking chair Dad used to sit on at our balcony back in Santo Domingo. I often reflect in it on the times we shared. I also kept his timeless DAKS jacket. Its smell reminds me of the man I looked up to as a beacon of decency and humility. I have always known that if only I could be half the man he had been, I would have amounted to something. Witnessing the dignity he maintained in the tragic situation of his final years was the most humbling experience of my life.

And another thing I have is the scrap of paper he directed me to with his last breath. Since 1993, when both my dad and Escobar died, there has been much speculation about the millions of dollars the drug lord was said to still possess at the time of his shooting. Many informants have reported it was buried somewhere for safekeeping. It has become the stuff of legend and worldwide interest.

Having seen for myself bags of cash Dad said came from Escobar's personal stash I know the legend is true. Since that day in Madrid it is clear the money has been moved. The clues to where are contained on that slip of paper. Over the years I have discovered the symbols are a Masonic code revealing the coordinates of the missing Escobar millions. Alas, I have not been able to crack the code and I have been left wondering whether Dad and a handful of his co-conspirators have managed to fool everyone as to its location.

Now I throw the challenge out to anyone willing to try and crack the enigma. Contained somewhere within the pages and on the cover of this book are the lines of code. Solve the mystery and the secret of Pablo Escobar's missing millions will finally be answered.

And if a portion of that recovered cash was put to good causes then the efforts of one intelligence agent who tried to walk a dangerous tightrope in a foreign land would not have been in vain.

ACKNOWLEDGMENTS

In writing this book I have had to take an incredibly difficult and on occasions extremely disturbing journey in to the past.

Without doubt, I could have never completed this arduous task without the help of some dear friends, family, and helpers.

Primarily I must thank my dear wife Julie for putting up with those many hours of having to listen to me read her the latest paragraphs in the unfolding saga that was my childhood. And for helping me to cope with dyslexia, and especially my terrible spelling.

A special thank you must also go to my editor Douglas Wight who somehow made sense of my ramblings and helped me turn my story into the book you see before you.

And finally, but by no means least, a special thank you to my publisher, for having the guts, determination and vision to take me on and make this happen.

Thank you.

Roberto Sendoya Escobar
(Phillip Witcomb)